I0415935

Cattails, Speckled Alders and Golden Tamaracks

Memories of Canine Companionship and Magic Moments in the Great Out-Of-Doors

By

Leon "Buckshot" Anderson

authorHOUSE™

1663 LIBERTY DRIVE, SUITE 200
BLOOMINGTON, INDIANA 47403
(800) 839-8640
WWW.AUTHORHOUSE.COM

This book is a work of non-fiction. Unless otherwise noted, the author and the publisher make no explicit guarantees as to the accuracy of the information contained in this book and in some cases, names of people and places have been altered to protect their privacy.

© 2005 Leon "Buckshot" Anderson. All Rights Reserved.

No part of this book may be reproduced, stored in a retrieval system, or transmitted by any means without the written permission of the author.

First published by AuthorHouse 03/16/05

ISBN: 1-4208-2256-X (sc)

Printed in the United States of America
Bloomington, Indiana

This book is printed on acid-free paper.

Dedication # 1

To "Andy", my dad, friend, companion and outdoor
teacher. Thanks Dad, for introducing me to the
wonderful world of Mother Nature!

Dedication # 2

To Old Pat, Duke, Teal, Maggie, Sadie, Siah, and Belle.
Without your obedient support, dedication and love, my
enjoyment in
the out doors would have been considerably less enjoyable!

Special Thanks

To "Ducks Unlimited" and all the loyal volunteers
and supporters who, since 1937 have donated millions of
dollars and worked millions of hours to protect our Nation's
valuable wetlands and marshes from development and
exploitation.

And Finally,

To my good friend and outdoor companion,
Dr. Thomas Tilkens, who acted as proofreader and friendly
critic.

"The outdoors holds many things of keen delight. A deer flashing across a burn, a squirrel corkscrewing up a tree trunk, a sharptail throbbing up from the stubble - all these have their place in my scheme of things. But the magic visitation of ducks from the sky to a set of bobbing blocks holds more of beauty and heart-pounding thrill than I have ever experienced afield with rod or gun. Not even the sure, hard pluck of a hard-to-fool brown trout, or the lurching smash of a river smallmouth has stirred me as has the circling caution of ducks coming to decoys."

Gordon MacQuarrie

"A dog is the only thing on Earth that loves you more than he loves himself"

Josh Billings

Introduction

"Cattails, Speckled Alders and Golden Tamaracks"

"Cattails, Speckled Alders and Golden Tamaracks" contains twenty true short stories, which highlight memorable outings the author has experienced over the past half-century. Primarily using wetland and marshes as the outdoor settings, these tales will immerse the reader in numerous remote, pristine places spanning much of the North American Continent.

Contained within are humorous, serious, life threatening, heart warming, tear jerking tales, which transport the reader from the watery wonderland that is Northern Wisconsin, to the open range of the Saint Johns River, coastal marshes, palmetto thickets, and Cyprus swamps of Central Florida. The voyage will continue to the prairie pothole region of the Great Plains as well as the marsh grass wetlands of Canada.

The staring roles are shared by the author's numerous outdoor friends, canine companions, and co-stars many of Ma Nature's creatures! The reader is introduced to ducks, geese, swans, various shorebirds, alligators, water moccasins, rattlesnakes, Brahma Bulls, and a host of other unlikely characters.

The bonding that occurs between master and dog is a central theme that is interwoven throughout the tales, as well as the way our human values concerning man's relationship with nature changes as our aging process advances.

The author's deep love and concern for the world's wild places is subtlety laced throughout the stories by "Buckshot" the Master Story Teller of the Northwood's"!

Table of Contents

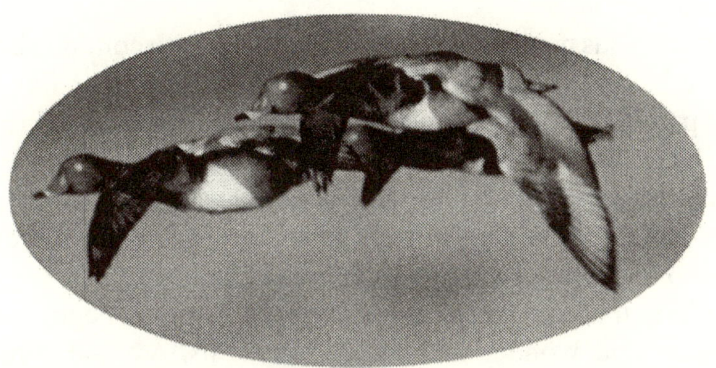

Forward

Hundreds of years before the advent of recorded history, when Homo Sapiens were primarily hunters and gatherers, man and wild dogs that had been domesticated forged a relationship geared mainly for the purpose of putting food on the stone table in their cave.
Over centuries of time, this man/dog relationship blossomed into a full-blown love affair.

It is not an accident or a quirk of history that dogs have been bestowed the deserved title of "man's best friend". Nothing could be more true or appropriate.

The twenty tales that follow are true. And although the central theme of each true store centers around the sport of waterfowling, there are much deeper and important messages being delivered. These are very personal stories about a journey from boyhood, to maturity, to middle age and beyond, of one man's relationship with his canine companions, his fellow outdoorsmen, and Ma Nature.

For hundreds of thousands of years earthlings only inhabited rural areas, as the concept of urban centers had not yet been invented. Man was simply a small cog in the scheme of nature, and like all the creatures big and small that inhabited the earth, man struggled to survive. Mankind was part of nature and adapted to the cards Mother Nature dealt.

Today, for the most part, all of that has changed. Today nature is generally forced to accept the changes brought about by man. And what has seemingly been good for man has all too frequently been disastrous for nature.

But what has not changed is man's inner urge to continue bonding with Ma Nature. Modern day humans still retain their link to the distant past by continuing to spend a great deal of time in the out of doors. Or at least longing to do so. Urban dwellers are of course at a disadvantage, compared to their counterparts who live in a rural setting. But still, the urge to sally forth and enjoy the wild areas is present to a greater or lesser degree in all mankind.

Nothing that man has built or invented can ever begin to match the beauty and wonder of Nature's creations. A vivid sunrise or sunset. An afternoon shower, which cools a muggy summer day. The raft of migrating geese etched upon a royal blue spring or fall sky. Or simply a relaxing walk with your dog and companions along a forest trail cushioned with dry autumn leaves. And there is so much more!

My personal love affair with the out of door can be explained with one simple explanation. I go because I enjoy the planning and the "going", and the just being there. The camaraderie experienced with my fellow outdoors persons and my canine companions are only overshadowed by my love of family. But the experiences and knowledge gained by bonding with Ma Nature rates a very close second!

In the Prolog, and the tales that follow, I'll make an attempt to explain what makes spending lots of time in the out of doors with Ma Nature and all her beautiful scenes and creatures so special. And in between the explaining, I'll share some of my most cherished memories about dogs, wild things, and moments in the great out of doors.

And through the six decades I have spent accumulating these memories, besides my outdoor companions and canine friends, most frequently my other companions were "Cattails, Speckled Alders, and Golden Tamaracks".

Enjoy the adventures!

Prolog: A Duck Hunt is.......

Time, unfortunately, stands still for no one. But, fortunately, we humans are able to store things, called "memory", in our gray matter. As Father Time causes our lives to race onward, it is often the pleasant memories of past events that continue to help make life beautiful. What follows are bits and pieces from my memory that has been stored from past outings in pursuit of pleasure. And the stories that follow represent some of my most cherished memories from the hundreds and hundreds of outdoor adventures I have been fortunate enough to experience over the past six decades.

The PROLOG for this collection of outdoor tales was one I wrote many years ago, simply to vent my inner most feeling about what, at least to me, makes the sport of duck hunting so very, very special.

Many, many years ago, it was 1945 to be exact, I was fortunate to find a life long friend named Eddie Petras. When Eddie moved from

Chicago to La Crosse, Wisconsin in the early 80's, he discovered a duck hunter's paradise. So it was that Eddie invited me to share a weeklong duck hunt in the fabled waterfowl marshes that comprise much of the Mississippi River basin in southwestern Wisconsin. How could I refuse? And while two very close friends sat in a duck blind, tucked neatly away in a thick stand of cattails, the idea for this narrative was born in my mind. Please enjoy sharing my personal emotions of what; "A Duck Hunt is...."

....

A duck hunt is;

Being awakened at 4:30 a.m. by a gentle but firm knock at your bedroom door, then pulling on warm wool clothing with a feeling of excitement and anticipation, followed by a hot cup of coffee being shoved into your hand, and a pleasant, but sleepy, "Good Morning!"

A duck hunt is;

Watching your Black Lab scamper to the boat dock, then a high-speed boat ride through inky pre-dawn blackness to claim "The Spot". During the ride there is bound to be the nuzzle of a warm, moist nose on your hand from an overeager retriever.

A duck hunt is;

Holding a flashlight while your host places three dozen decoys in "just the right set up". It's an hour's wait under twinkling stars, or possibly listening to raindrops pitter-patter on your rain suit, or maybe even some snowflakes splatter on your face. It's soft toned conversation between friends, interrupted by sips of hot coffee, as you wait for the pink blush of dawn to soften the eastern horizon.

A duck hunt is;

Hearing the rush of air over feathered wings by an unseen flock of early risers, as they wing their way to some distant feeding grounds, followed by a gentle whine from your four legged companion, she has heard them too!
It's looking for the hundredth time at your watch and noting that shooting time is now only five minutes away, and feeling a quickening of your heart as three number two steel duck loads are fed into your faithful Remington 870.

ii

A duck hunt is;

It's hearing the morning's first shot fired by someone who forgot to set his watch. He's four minutes too early. It's feeling your heartbeat quicken by seeing that first black blob suddenly take shape as a duck. It's reacting to instinct as your partner says "Take Him", and watching a drake mallard fold neatly and tumble into the decoys. It's a feeling of pride as your "old pro" makes her first retrieve of the morning. It's hearing your hunting partner say, "Nice shot, at least we're not skunked!" It's feeling the day is a success, even if you don't fire another shot!

A duck hunt is;

Seeing the earth come to life as the sun steadily beats back the night's darkness, and watching blackbirds, crows, herons, muskrats and other members of God's community start another day.

A duck hunt is;

Congratulating your friend after he makes an outstanding shot on a high flying blue bill, then being surprised by a low flying flock of teal, which buzz your decoys, without a shot being fired.

Or having a pair of baldpates almost work into range and then flair off for higher altitude.

And later, feeling slight embarrassment after listening to your host call a drake pintail into point blank range, and then missing him with all three shots.

A duck hunt is;

Sharing your last sandwich with your retriever, and finishing the last of your lukewarm coffee.

It's a slight feeling of sadness as the decoys are picked up and stored until tomorrow.

It's walking into a warm, cozy house and pulling off a pair of soggy waders.

It's giving extra rations to the one who worked the hardest, and a pat on the head for a job well done. Then watching her curl up by the fireplace and fall asleep.

A duck hunt is;

An icy glass of Southern Comfort before supper. Maybe two. And after dinner reliving the day's highlights prior to turning in for the night at 9:30. Four-thirty will come quickly.

It's falling into bed feeling totally spent, but also feeling your body smile all over, as your mind replays the memory of that first mallard of the morning once again falling into the decoys.

A duck hunt is;

Feeling the warmth of a down quilt as you snuggle into bed, and hoping tomorrow will be cloudy and windy. And just before being enveloped by sound, peaceful sleep, it's thanking God he gave you this day, this friendship. and these memories!

It's a duck hunt!

Catching the Fever

Life is full of "firsts". Most firsts are of little importance and generally the memory of the event or situation quickly fades away or becomes relegated to the most remote corners of our memory banks. But there are, and always will be, certain first's that remain indelibly ingrained in our box of recollections forever! Such an event occurred to me on the first Saturday of October in 1948, and it changed the course of my outdoor exploits for life!

****

The double-barreled twenty gauge arrived under our Christmas Tree in 1947. Uncle Bud had ordered it from Montgomery Ward, which caused his wallet to shrink by an amount of $49.95. He broke the gun down into its three component parts, stock & receiver, forearm, and barrels. Then he wrapped each part separately and put my name on each package.

By the lights of the small flickering candles used to decorate our tree, I tore open the packages on Christmas Eve and discovered what at that time was the "treasure of a lifetime". Uncle Bud's little trick worked too, as it took me a few seconds after tearing off the wrapping paper to realize exactly had I had been given. My joy was so overwhelming that I actually shed a few joyous tears. Next to dad and mom, Uncle Bud was my favorite person in the whole world, even before I got the gun.

It was a Stevens Model 311. Wartime shortages had even effected the firearms industry and my new weapon had a stock and forearm made of plastic. But that did make it lighter, and for an eighty five-pound stringbean, that was a good thing.

My acquisition of that new 20 gauge doubled the number of guns I owned, so my tiny Stevens single shot .410 suddenly was thrust into being "second best". However, my instructors limited my freedom to start toting that new gun after squirrels and rabbits, so for several more seasons my trusty .410 still saw lots of time in the woods.

By fall of the year following the arrival of the 20 gauge, dad deemed I was ready to be his partner for the opening day of duck season, which traditionally fell on the first Saturday in October. For several weeks prior to the opening I was so excited I could hardly sleep. And even though the waiting period included a three day camping and grouse hunting trip into the vast Nicolet National Forest, my waking hours were consumed with speculation and anticipation about the upcoming duck season.

The Conservation Department of the State of Wisconsin has been kind enough to ease the ducks into duck season with some degree of gentleness. Legal shooting time on opening day begins at noon. From then on the opening salvos may begin a half-hour before sunrise, when the duck hunter has a huge advantage. Hunters can see incoming waterfowl outlined against a morning sky, but the ducks have a difficult time spotting camouflaged hunters concealed in their blinds on the ground. The noon hour opening does allow the lucky younger ducks, which escape the opening day surprise, to "wise up" a bit.

Dad's chosen opening day hot spot was a marshy segment of Squaw Creek, which was about twenty-five miles west of where we lived. (And, I still do) We arrived at the fabled marsh about ten thirty a.m. and took our time constructing a make shift blind out of marsh grass and cattails, which were woven into the branches of the speckled alders that lined the stream's banks. After construction was completed and approved by my instructor, he waded out into the water and professionally positioned a dozen or so decoys in "just the right set up".

The day was one that could be referred to as "perfect Indian Summer". A royal blue sky, with a few fleecy cumulous clouds thrown in for contrast, provided us with a roof, and warming rays of a smiling Old Sol made the temperature such that heavy garments were not necessary. A gentle southwest breeze rippled the surface of Squaw Creek, making our decoys swim left and right almost as natural as a flock of feeding ducks. The frost bitten leaves of the cattails chattered to each other with each puff of breeze. The boggy shoreline was dotted with tamaracks, which were in their early stages of changing from summer green to the gold of autumn. The setting was spectacular, but for me, each minute of the final half-hour of waiting seemed to take a century! Even our retriever, Old Pat, a black cocker spaniel with several years of experience under his collar, squirmed, looked skyward, and whined. He too was anxious for action!

At exactly twelve noon, dad shot a grin in my direction, snapped open the receiver of his Lefever double barreled twelve gauge, dropped in two number six Remington Express Duck Loads, and said, "Load her up Buckshot, it's time to do some shooting."

We didn't have long to wait. From further north along the river a burst of gunfire announced the season was officially open! A small group of black dots appeared just over the horizon and quickly materialized into ducks, which were following the twisting path of Squaw Creek.

Dad quickly resumed the role of teacher, and hunching down more deeply into our blind whispered a hushed command. "Don't move and don't look up. I'll tell you when to take 'um."

At dad's command of "Now", he and I rose to test our marksmanship. The black ducks spotted our movement and flared upward. Dad's long barreled Lefever barked twice, and two plump birds fell from the sky.

In an instant Old Pat was heading across the creek in pursuit of dad's ducks. Dad looked questioningly at me and asked, "Why didn't you shoot?"

I'm sure my eyes were bulging out of their sockets as I managed a feeble answer. "Heck dad, those ducks were moving so fast,......why,......by the time I got my gun up they were already out of range!"

Dad patted me on the back and tried to sooth my disappointment. "Ya, they can move all right. But you'll get the hang of it before the afternoons over. You'll get some shooting in."

I was a bit worried about his reply, although he promised I'd get in some shooting, he said nothing about hitting one of those feathered rockets.

For the next half-hour I received advanced instruction about "Lead", and "Swing", and "Follow Through". Dad illustrated his instruction by using his shotgun as a pointer, using lead, swing and follow through at imaginary ducks. Then he had me practice the same moves. Now for sure I was primed and ready for action!

By three thirty dad had his limit. Three chunky black ducks and a blue winged teal. I had a half dozen empty 20-gauge casings. And a sad look on my face!

Dad put his gun in his case and more instruction about lead, swing, and follow through took place. It didn't help my spirits one bit! I was sure I'd go home from my first ever duck hunt,......SKUNKED!

Another hour passed. The sky remained empty of ducks. I kept myself busy by whittling a wooden knife from a chunk of dead alder. And then it happened!

Dad, who had been standing and acting as my lookout, suddenly grabbed my shoulder and whispered, "Get down! Here comes a whole flock of teal"!

His pointing finger led my eyes to a fast moving blob of beating wings. At first I thought I was looking at another of the many flocks of red winged blackbirds that had been cruising up and down Squaw Creek all afternoon. Dad gave me a suggestion. "Pick out one bird and remember what I showed you about lead, swing and follow through!" And seconds later came the final order. "Now!"

I raised up from my crouched position, firmly settling the butt of my new twenty on my shoulder as I rose. Before me was a squadron of about twenty blue winged teal, flying at a speed just short of breaking the sound barrier. The sound made by the rush of air over their wings and bodies sounded like a P-51 Mustang in a power dive!

My mind became vacant, and any thoughts of lead, swing, or follow through remained somewhere in it's vacuum. I aimed in the general direction of the lead birds and jerked the front trigger. To my utter amazement, the last bird in the flock folded up as though it had hit a stone wall and landed in the cattails on the far side of the creek! Once again, my eyes nearly popped out of their sockets!

"Hey, nice shot Buckshot!", was the reaction from my beaming father. "You did it right that time!"

And believe me, I didn't confess I had actually "flock shot". But a few weeks later I did confess. Dad laughed.

Several minutes later Old Pat dropped the small bird at my feet. I patted his wet head about a dozen times and told him what a great dog he was. But Old Pat already knew that. I turned the bird over and over in my hands and realized I had suddenly become a duck hunter,......just like dad!

Well, we came home with five ducks that memorable day. We stayed in the blind for another hour or so, and then by mutual consent, picked up the decoys and called it a day.

Dad took me duck hunting a couple more times that fall, but I missed the few ducks I had a chance to shoot at. But more importantly,......I had contracted "The Fever"!

A Devine Greenhead

Throughout our Nation's Duck Hunting Fraternity there is nearly unanimous agreement that the most popular duck, which is also the most populous on the North American Continent, is the common mallard. And the male of the species is unquestionably the "King"!

Mallards are large, as ducks go, numerous, and last but not least, tasty. Presently, they are found from coast to coast in abundant numbers and are able to adapt to a wide variety of varied environments. They can be found from the most remote marshes and prairie potholes to the parks and lagoons of our largest cities. Mallards have even been known to nest near swimming pools in crowded urban settings. But it wasn't always this way.

During my growing up years in the 1940's and 50's, the vast watersheds of Northern Wisconsin contained limited numbers of common mallards. Our most common duck was the black duck, a close relative of the mallard. Local nimrods generally referred to the black duck as "black mallards".

The bagging of my first duck, which was chronicled in "Catching the Fever", remains as one of my mind's most vivid and cherished memories. So too is the memory of bagging my first greenhead!

After bagging but one duck, that unlucky blue winged teal in the fall of 1948, by the following season I had matured greatly. (At least in my own mind.) Also, my shooting ability improved somewhat, due to continued instruction concerning "lead", "swing" and "follow through". By the close of duck season in 1949 my personal score board boasted the number "six". Mathematically, that's a tremendous increase! But still, no common mallards showed up in the statistics.

During the season of 1950 I bagged my first mallard, a young hen. But those magnificent emerald green headed drakes continued to be harder to collect than gold nuggets. My season total swelled to eight birds, and although it was a modest gain, my success was headed in the right direction.

I looked forward to October of 1951with a sizable increase of anticipation and determination.

****

Although not totally unexpected, dad's announcement that I would be included in his annual "Opening Weekend Camping and Duck Hunting Expedition" created an emotional outburst rivaling that which occurred when dad allowed me to go with him on my first deer hunt!

During the fall of 1949 dad and several of his duck hunting cronies somehow gained information about "The Mother of all Duck Hunting Marshes". An extensive exploration of the rumored fabled area resulted in the beginning of an annual outing to that marsh, which continued for five consecutive duck season opening weekends.

The marsh was located in an extensive low-lying area, which surrounded Devine Lake. The lake itself is a shallow depression in the earth that Ma Nature saw fit to fill with rich, black muck. The lakeshore is surrounded by a boggy, cattail infested floating bog, interspersed with speckled alders and tamaracks. Much of the lake's shallow muddy areas contained dense stands of wild rice, which for ducks ranks as one of their top dining choices.

Rounding out the geographical configuration of the Devine Lake Marsh, are two large side springs, which deposit just the right amount and quality of water into the lake, adding considerably to its rice growing ability. And last but not least, an island about five acres in size covered with balsam, white birch, maple and a few pines, occupies the southeast corner of the lake.

Early on the morning of the first Saturday in October of 1951 a two-vehicle convoy headed west on highway 70 towards what I had been promised would be a duck hunter's paradise. I was not to be disappointed.

Dad, driving our aging 1941 Chevy pickup was in the lead. Toby Andersen, a duck hunter, which if such a thing existed as a Duck Hunter's Hall of Fame would certainly have been an inductee, occupied the passenger seat. I was perched upon Toby's lap. Our black cocker spaniel, Old Pat, was scrunched in between Dad and Toby panting with anticipation. Following the lead vehicle was an ancient panel truck, driven by Deloyd and Charlie Goodyear, both duck hunting novices. Beside five eager hunters and one nearly ballistic dog, both vehicles were packed to capacity with camping and hunting paraphernalia.

The final mile of our sixteen-mile trip was on what vaguely resembled a road, which wound through a forest of mixed hardwoods and scattered pine. The so-called road ended abruptly at the crest of a high, steep valley, which housed a small trout stream named Mishonagon Creek.

All our equipment, which was quite substantial, was carried down the hill to the bank of the babbling brook. The final items to be dragged down the steep embankment were the watercraft which would ultimately carry us and our gear to our campsite, and later to our duck blinds.

Charlie and Deloyd rode in a vintage seventeen-foot Old Town canvas covered cedar strip canoe. Toby used a twelve-foot wooden duck skiff, the forerunner of today's kayaks. Dad, Old Pat and I, plus the majority of our camping gear occupied a fourteen-foot flat-bottomed metal rowboat. Dad called it "The Tub".

Our upstream journey towards Devine Lake was also not without major difficulties. The first two hundred yards consisted of shallow sand and gravel riffles, making it necessary to physically pull our overloaded craft against the current. Then came the beaver dam! On a scale of one to ten, this baby was a fifteen! Dad called it "The Hoover Dam of the Mishonagon". With much huffing and puffing our three-overloaded watercraft were lifted up and over the dam. From then on it was clear sailing all the way to our chosen campsite on the island.

By eleven a.m. our camp site was ship shape. Dad's eight by eight-foot canvas tent was nestled securely within the confines of a balsam thicket just a few feet from the waters edge. The floor of the tent had been covered with a mattress of balsam boughs nearly a foot and a half thick. We would sleep soundly and comfortably, and hopefully the sweet smelling balsam would mask the musty smell of that old canvas tent!

A half hour later the over eager hunters were nestled in their respective blinds, counting off the minutes until noon, when legal shooting time would begin another duck season.

Dad's gang did well. Without too much effort we departed the Devine Lake Marsh late Sunday afternoon with a full two day limit which included black ducks, teal, ring necks and several mallards. Dad and Toby had each bagged a greenhead, but my earlier dream of bagging one of those then rare and beautiful birds had been dashed on the jagged rocks of despair.

I continued to hunt ducks nearly ever moment I was free to do so for the remaineder the 1951 season, and although my total count climbed to eighteen, with two of those birds being mallards, still there had been no greenhead! I began to think I'd live my entire duck hunting life without ever reaching the greenhead milestone.

The first Saturday in October of 1952 marked the beginning of my fifth season as a duck hunter. Now a veteran at age fifteen, I was more than determined to harvest a greenhead. But still that dreaded dark and foreboding shadow of doubt lurked in my sub-conscience.

Dad's gang of duck hunters once again took part in what was the Third Annual Devine Lake Expedition. Deloyd dropped out of the group, for reasons unknown, and with a considerable amount of prodding, Uncle Bud agreed to join our ranks. Also missing from the occasion was our black cocker spaniel, Old Pat.

As he had aged, so had advanced his arthritic condition. Spending time in icy cold water and sleeping in an unheated tent was not a good combination for an old dog with arthritis. So mom and dad had made a decision that our retriever would remain home and help mom keep the home fires burning.

Two weeks prior to the season opener, dad and Toby ventured into the marsh and constructed our duck blinds. Dad selected a new location near the mouth of one of the small spring streams that flowed into Devine Lake from one of the spring systems. The previous year dad had noted the incoming ducks seemed to like that area, so his decision to move us from our blind on the island to the boggy shore was done for a good reason. But, there was a negative factor, which we were quick to discover shortly after noon on opening day.

Dad had fashioned a blind out of two rows of alder branches stuck in the mud and interwoven with marsh grass and cattails. The Tub could be shoved in between the rows of camouflage and dad and I could relax in the comfort of our boat while we waited for the ducks to arrive over our decoys.

Shortly after the magical legal hour arrived the faint sound of gunfire far to our north reached our ears. Within several minutes a large flight of ducks appeared on the horizon headed straight for the Devine Lake Marsh. It was a massive flock made up mainly of black ducks. Our pulse rate quickened as the birds drew nearer and nearer.

The huge flock numbered several hundred. As it passed over Devine Lake at high altitude, the mass began to break up into smaller flocks, which began circling ever lower and lower looking for just the right spot to stop in for an afternoon snack of wild rice.

As my watering eyes peered through our screen of camo watching the show taking place over the rice beds before me, a sudden sharp whispered warning came from dad.

"Behind us! Just over the tamaracks! Blacks coming in!"

I quickly turned and saw over a dozen giant birds, "flaps" down, wings cupped, and landing gears being lowered. Dad whispered, "Take 'um!"

As I raised up one bird among the black ducks caught my eye. A gray belly, a chestnut breast and a head of emerald green glistened in the afternoon sun! A greenhead!

The barrels of my little twenty gauge swung to the front of his bill, I hesitated a split second to move my finger from the front trigger which would tough off the modified barrel and jerked the rear trigger, which controlled the full choke barrel.

What at the time seemed like slow motion, the drake mallard folded up as cleanly as any duck I had ever shot. He tumbled end over end in a continuous motion and landed with an audible "plop" in a clump of cattails. I was so surprised and thrilled I never touched off my second barrel at another duck! But I did mentally mark the EXACT spot where my long sought after prize had crash-landed!

Not surprisingly, dad had dropped two black ducks with his Lefever double. "Did you get any?", he asked, a wide grin spreading across his weather beaten face.

I swallowed a lump that had formed in my throat, and tried to act nonchalant. "Ya, I killed a greenhead."

The handshake and the thump on my back are remembered as well as the vision of my first greenhead folding up stone cold dead. But my moment of glory was short lived.

Upon attempting to reach my greenhead and one of dad's black ducks, both of which had fallen into the cattail bog about thirty yards from The Tub, we discovered big trouble. The spongy surface of the bog was so thin even my one hundred-pound body broke through into was seemed to be a bottomless mass of muck.

Several different approaches were attempted, but to no avail. There was no safe way for a human to reach those downed ducks! And the answer to our dilemma was home with mom!

The afternoon dragged. Dad and I had to make sure any ducks we shot were out in front of our blind where they would fall into the water so they could be retrieved by rowing out with The Tub. My depression deepened. But although he hadn't yet informed me, dad had figured out how we were going to get my greenhead and his black duck. Never, would he ever consider giving up on retrieving and using something we had shot and killed!

We picked up our decoys two hours before legal shooting time ended due to the fact we had "limited out". And that was counting the two birds that still remained unclaimed in the bog. Back at our campsite dad partially filled me in on how we were going to get those two missing ducks.

"I'm going to make a trip back home and get something we need to retrieve those ducks. It'll be dark before I get back, so start a fire before Toby, Charlie and Uncle Bud get back. Take the guts out of our ducks and stuff their cavity full of sphagnum moss like I showed ya. Then hang 'um up by their necks in a tree to cool. Don't wait supper on me, I'll be back as soon as I can."

And off he rowed, heading down Mishonagon Creek. I scratched my head, wondering what dad was going home to get, and decided he was going to bring Old Pat back with him. I mean, how else could we get those ducks?

Shortly after dusk settled in the remaining trio of hunters returned. Toby had a limit, which was no surprise, and Uncle Bud and Charlie were two birds short of their limit.

I filled my companions in on what had transpired which caused dad's absence. They, like me, figured dad would return with Old Pat, arthritis or no arthritis. Time continued to drag.

The temperature cooled rapidly with deepening darkness. Fog began to settle over the lake. Stars twinkled above and a multitude of night sounds began to break the stillness. To the west a great horned owl hooted the welcome darkness, as it prepared for it's nighttime hunt. Not to be outdone, a coyote yelped somewhere to our south. It sure was peaceful sitting by a crackling fire, listening to my adult friends tell stories of hunts past.

I was getting pretty sleepy and thinking about crawling under my massive pile of blankets on our mattress of balsam boughs when we detected the rhythmic squeak of dad's oars as he rowed The Tub towards our campsite across the fog shrouded surface of Devine Lake. I was excited about having Old Pat curl up with me under the blankets.

Amidst a hail of friendly greetings The Tub was pulled ashore. Dad stepped out into the ring of firelight, but Old Pat did not follow.

"Where's our dog?", I asked with a puzzled look on my face.

"He's back home with your ma."

"I thought you went home to bring Pat back so he could find our ducks tomorrow morning."

'Nope, no dog. But I've got something that YOU can use to fetch our ducks." And dad pulled his pair of long pickerel style snowshoes out of the boat.

"We'll put these on your feet and you'll be able to walk anywhere on that bog you'd like to walk."

I was skeptical, but knew better than to doubt dad's ability to figure out the answer to a puzzle. If he said snowshoes would hold me up on that treacherous bog, then they'd hold me up. But as I snuggled under my blankets and closed my eyes, a whole bunch of new fears danced through my brain.

I knew a marsh literally crawls with predators and scavengers during the nighttime hours. And any one of a half dozen or more could devour my greenhead or chew it to pieces, or drag it off someplace where it would never be found. There were raccoons, mink, otters, fox, coyotes, skunks and who knew what else out there looking for an easy meal! Sleep did not come easy, nor did I experience sound sleep.

The sound of someone splitting kindling awoke me at five a.m. As soon as the fire was roaring I grabbed my cold clothes and huddled near that wonderful fire with it's radiating warmth and dressed as rapidly as possible. Dad cooked up a massive pile of bacon, thick sliced ham, fried potatoes and scrambled eggs. The adults inhaled several cups of scalding coffee, while I mixed up a cup of hot cocoa.

Dad and I were back in our blind a half-hour before legal shooting time. As usual, daylight crept in like a chilled snail. Sunsets can be breathtakingly beautiful, but nothing, and I mean nothing, can beat the beauty and wonderment of a sunrise over a wildlife marsh. Watching the black of night slowly soften as the pink, then orange, and finally the yellow glow of morning creeps over the landscape is a sight I never tire of watching.

And nearly every morning hunters will hear a sound that will cause goose bumps to rise on the skin of even a veteran of many hunts. The sound of air rushing over the wings of an unseen flock of early risers as they wing their way off to some morning gathering point to feed. And even though we hunters know we won't see them,.....we look skyward anyway!

As soon as it was light enough to see fairly well, I began asking dad if I could put on the snowshoes and look for my greenhead,..........and his black duck. I figured what he'd say, and I was right.

"No, not yet. The first half-hour or so of shooting time is generally the most productive. You can look for those ducks after the early morning shooting slows down."

And so it was. With the arrival of legal shooting time the shooting began. Flock after flock of ducks circled the marsh, got shot at and then left for parts unknown. About a quarter after seven I received permission to begin playing retriever.

My first couple of steps were made with a great deal of dread. What if dad was wrong? What if I busted through the bog with those cumbersome snowshoes strapped to my boots? Why, I'd probably sink out of sight in seconds and pop up somewhere in China.

I looked back at dad, and as usual,.....he was grinning from ear to ear. "Go on. Go get that greenhead you've been worrying about all night!"

His remark hit me like a sledgehammer! How did he know I was worried? But then again,.......why should I be surprised he had felt what I was feeling. Dads and moms seem to be able to do just that all too often!

Reassured that dad's snowshoes would indeed hold me up as I squished my way across the bog, my eyes riveted on the clump of cattails which had made a permanent impression in my brain about eighteen hours earlier. I actually had seen the cattails wiggle when my long awaited prize had plummeted into their midst.

Once reaching my destination, I hesitated parting the leaves to look for my duck. I was almost afraid to look for fear my worst fears would come true. I grabbed a handful of cattail stalks, closed my eyes, and bent the stalks to one side. Then I opened one eye. There rested a greenhead mallard, breast up, feet extended and neck outstretched. I opened my other eye. The duck was still there. He looked as thought someone had gently laid him on a bed of marsh grass. Maybe "somebody" did!

I reached down, picked him up by his neck and turned around holding him high for dad to view. His grinning face beamed even more brightly and he loudly applauded. That's the kind of dad I had!

I took a bit longer to find the black duck, as dad was shooting at another bird when the first one fell. So he didn't actually see where the first one landed. But I found it. Not as quickly or gracefully as Old Pat would have, but I got it.

By noon we had our limit. No other greenheads were taken, and although it was selfish to feel so, I was happy. I had the only one brought back to camp that day! Wasn't I the hero?

It was nearing four p.m. before all our gear had been dragged back up that terrible steep hill and loaded aboard our vehicles. Once safely home again, our daily bag was cleaned, wrapped and tucked in our freezer. Throughout the long winter months numerous mouth watering roasted duck dinners awaited us.

I can still recall picking the feathers off my first greenhead. After removing most of the feathers, dad dipped the birds in hot, melted paraffin wax, then he dunked them in cold water to harden the wax. When the wax was removed from the ducks, all the down and pin feathers remained in the wax, resulting in a duck with perfectly clean skin! After this final step, I counted the pellet holes in my greenhead. There were seventeen! Dad said, "Looks like you centered him." And I guess maybe I did.

The annual outing to Devine Lake continued through the season of 1954. In September of 1955 the junior member of the gang drifted off to college and for reasons unknown to me, the annual pilgrimage to the Devine Lake Marsh came to an end. I guess one could say "An era had ended".

The memories of those four annual outings, of which I was a member, are still fresh in my mind even though a half-century has evaporated. The companionship I experienced with dad, Uncle Bud, Charlie, Deloyd and Toby were great learning experiences. They were friends and teachers of the highest caliber. All youngsters need adult guidance, and what better classroom is there but the one designed by Ma Nature?

If I close my eyes and let my memory wander back in time I can still hear the stories which were told around an evening camp fire, smell the balsam and the smoke from our campfire, hear the laughter, and once again see a greenhead tumbling to earth. And like a favorite video recording, I watch and listen to it often!

Lost Creek; "My Training Ground"

For a youngster to progress in any endeavor requires four basic ingredients, good teachers, time, a classroom, and possibly above all else, a sincere, burning desire by the student to learn and improve his or her skills.

My teachers were all far above being just run of the mill outdoorsmen.

Time was often in somewhat short supply, but my teachers always seemed to be willing to squeeze a little of it out now and then for purposes of instruction.

The classroom, which surrounded my home, stretched for miles in every direction, having been designed by the greatest outdoor designer of all time, Ma Nature.

And if my youthful desire to learn how to hunt, fish, trap and do all the rest that goes with living an "outdoor life" could have been converted to cash, I'd have been a multi-millionaire!

The majority of my early lessons concerning duck hunting took place very close to our home. Lost Creek, a rare jewel of nature, which was created by the melting glaciers ten thousand years earlier, flowed through a portion of our personal one hundred and twenty acres of pristine wilderness. Approximately five miles in length, it originates in Lost Lake and meanders through a variety of different types of terrain to deposit its water in Big St. Germain Lake.

Along its twisting course one can find intermittent sand and gravel riffles, interspersed with wide, shallow, muddy sections filled with various types of delicious food for wild creatures of all kinds. And best of all, at the time during my early educational sessions, the only homes along its banks were several where it left Lost Lake and entered Big St. Germain Lake!

It was here I learned to blow a duck call, (although a half century later much of my calling still silences all God's creatures for several miles) how to distinguish different species of waterfowl, improve my wing shooting, and how to belly crawl through muck and mire to get in range of a flock of wary mallards, black ducks, wood ducks or teal.

The "family duck blind" has been moved to several different locations over the past sixty plus seasons, but come opening day, as long as my body and mind allow,....I'll be there, wherever it is, to continue my education!

✳✳

Dad helped me construct our first duck blind on the outside of the first bend below the third set of riffles. Just to our left, a tiny rivulet of icy spring water, which originated on our property, trickled into Lost Creek. Here the creek widened considerably, the current slowed, and a treasure trove of water plants beckoned waterfowl from miles around to come, settle in, relax and feed. It was a dandy location and I was able to hunt from its concealment for nearly forty seasons.

Actually, the property on which we built that first blind was on an eighty acre parcel belonging to a couple from Illinois. Dad became the caretaker of the land, as Ed and Millie only spent a few weeks each summer at their small log cabin on Dollar Lake. The members of the Anderson Family had free run of the land all year long. But that came to an end in the late 70's when the property changed owners.

My earliest attempts at "stalking", or using duck hunter's lingo, "sneaking up on" ducks, generally ended in disaster. To be honest, my major weakness in accomplishing this often-difficult task was simply, "being clumsy". My clumsiness was largely the result of being in too much of a hurry to get in range for a shot or two.

If there was a dry twig in my path, I'd make it snap. If the speckled alders were thick along my route to the feeding ducks, I'd bump them hard enough to make them shake and quiver. Generally the ducks knew I was coming well before I could get in range. But, I had a solution to my early over eagerness.

Dad owned a small sawmill. And one of the by-products of the lumber he produced was several huge piles of sawdust. With the aid of a wheelbarrow, I spent many hours wheeling many loads of sawdust the quarter mile to the creek and constructing several "sneaking trails", which I paved with sawdust. And it worked!

But as I slowly matured and became better at quelling my anxiousness, I became a genuine Daniel Boone at sneaking up on ducks. And for many seasons, it was my favorite method of bagging a few duck dinners.

One of my head instructors, Uncle Bud, was also an expert carpenter. Bud could make anything that required wood as the basic material. And one of his favorite building projects was constructing wooden fishing boats.

When I was fourteen, a huge Christmas present arrived under the tree from Uncle Bud to me. It was an eight-foot wooden duck skiff! Hand crafted from marine plywood with an oak frame and ribs, it was a thing of beauty! Fore and Aft were flat covered decks, under which one could store all kinds of hunting stuff. Our black cocker spaniel, Old Pat, had room to ride on the front deck while his young companion paddled the skiff up and down Lost Creek in quest of quackers.

On October week ends, and often well into November, Dad would load my skiff in the back of his '41 Chevy pickup and haul me and Old Pat to where the creek made its exit from Lost Lake. The downstream trip from there to our property was about three miles of wilderness, with the possibility of crossing paths with ducks at every bend!

It did not take too many trips for the student and his companion to map out a strategy that paid many dividends for many seasons. Keeping close to the banks on the inside of the bends, and glassing the water ahead, I was more often than not able to spot the resting or feeding ducks before they saw me. Then I'd carefully and quietly beach the skiff, command Old Pat to "heal", and together we'd make the sneak. Old Pat and I got lots of ducks that way and we developed into, as dad liked to say, "A well-oiled machine".

Also, often I'd blunder into a flock while zipping through the shallow riffles. Then I had to drop my paddle, pick up the shotgun, and shoot at the birds from a moving craft before they got out of range. But I had more success with the sneak method.

Old Pat, at age fourteen, made his last retrieve on Lost Creek during our last duck hunting expedition together.

Home from college for a weekend during my freshman year, I just had to revisit my favorite duck hunting spot. Dad dropped us off at the usual beginning point and Old Pat and I entered paradise.

Downstream less than a half mile I spotted three wood ducks feeding quietly along the east bank of the marshy shoreline several hundred yards ahead of me. The sneak was an easy one. Our route took us through a thickly forested swamp filled with black spruce and golden tamaracks. The floor of the wetlands was covered with sphagnum moss, making our approach deathly quiet.

Finally maneuvering within fifty yards of the unsuspecting trio, I stopped and pointed to the ground behind me, which was my silent signal to Old Pat to "sit and stay". He would faithfully obey and stay put until I shot. Then he'd come flying to my side, with those long, black, curly ears a floppin' like he was trying to actually fly. God, he was a good dog!

Leaving my companion behind I made the final approach. The shoreline lacked vegetation and the sharp-eyed woodies spotted me as I raised up to shoot. But they were close, and my two shots cleanly dropped the two drakes. The hen departed to search out new boy friends and a quieter location in which to feed.

Several seconds ticked off, but Old Pat did not arrive at the scene to finish our job. I called for him. Still no dog appeared. My bewilderment changed to fear. An unanswered question raced through my mind. "Did something happen to my faithful retriever? Why won't he come?"

I quickly retraced my steps to find Old Pat still sitting exactly where I had left him. At my arrival he wagged his tail so hard his butt wiggled with it. I stopped a dozen feet short of him and called again. Still he stayed put.

I thought maybe he had stepped in a trap and couldn't move. But that was out of the question or he'd have been howling his head off. I walked to his side and kneeled down asking him, "What's the matter boy?" Those big brown friendly eyes looked into mine but offered no answer to my question.

Then the truth struck me. My best pal for fourteen-years had become deaf! Stone cold deaf!

He followed me to where I had bagged my two ducks, and although I pointed and told him to "fetch", he simply sat by my side and looked confused. Then I tossed a stick towards the floating wood ducks and he understood the message I was trying to convey to him.

As Old Pat made his last two retrieves I sat down, leaned my back against a tamarack tree and balled my head off. And I'm not ashamed to say so!

Later that winter, while mom and dad were visiting friends in Chicago, Old Pat squeezed out of their car through a partly open window and disappeared. My folks stayed in the city for several extra days, spending hours and hours combing the neighborhood looking for our missing family member. They even ran ads in the newspaper. But he was gone!

Their letter arrived at my dorm in Superior several days after the search for Old Pat had been abandoned. I cried a whole bunch then too! But the memories of our fourteen wonderful years we spent together continue, and Old Pat was the first of many, many damn good dogs I've hunted with,....and loved!

"Toby"

Along the twisting path of life everyone can discover any number of what might be labeled, "special people". For me, Toby Andersen was one such individual.

Toby, who was a mechanical engineer by trade, grew up in Green Bay, Wisconsin. At that time the marshes which comprised much of the shoreline along the vast stretches of Green Bay were legendary as waterfowl areas. The duck-hunting bug bit Toby at an early age and throughout his life he often stated that duck hunting remained as his favorite outdoor activity.

Toby and his wife, Dottie, moved to Vilas County about the time World War II came to a close and bought a small resort on the north shore of Big St. Germain Lake. My dad and mom, Andy and Esther, soon became close friends with the Andersen's

As mentioned in an earlier tale, "A DEVINE GREENHEAD", Toby was one of the charter members of my dad's gang of duck hunters. And as a duck hunter, Toby had no equal.

He preferred to hunt alone, although he did hunt with a partner occasionally. I was given a number of opportunities to share time with Toby in a duck blind, or doing some "jump shooting" from his canoe. And each and every adventure offered up great memories and a new learning experience!

Toby toted an old square back Browning semi-auto loaded with Remington Nitro-Express or Peter's High Velocity duck loads. And when he pulled the trigger and made his Browning bark feathered fowl fell from the sky! Rarely did he miss! His marksmanship with a scattergun was uncanny!

Unlike my dad, who was also rated highly above average when it came to dropping game birds from the sky, Toby used a different style of shooting. Dad was a "lead", swing, and follow through" shooter. Toby was a "point and shoot" shooter. And it was he who realized that I too was a natural "pointer". And it was he who convinced me to give up the lead, swing, and follow through technique that dad had pounded into my head. Immediately my success on hitting flying objects improved tremendously.

Toby was tall and wiry, with a crop of immaturely gray hair which sat atop a head supporting a finely chiseled, handsome, distinguished face. Easy going and generally smiling, he was an easy person to get to know and even easier to take a strong liking to.

His talents were many, his shortcomings few, if any. Toby did some minor gunsmithing, which included converting my little Stevens .410 single barrel, which had been manufactured to only accept two and a half inch shells, to one which could also shoot the more powerful three inch ammunition.

He produced magnificent cedar strip rowing boats, which were highly prized by local guides and "row trollers". I know of several still in use to this day!

His hand made decoys were masterpieces. Often he used but a half dozen giant sized black duck decoys he had skillfully carved out of white cedar. More than once other hunters mistook his fakes for the real thing!

One of his favorite set-ups to dupe some ducks was accomplished quite simply. Toby would cover the bow and aft decks of his duck skiff with marsh grass, cattails, or wild rice plants. Then he'd paddle out to a large muskrat house, put out his half dozen black duck decoys, and hunker down behind the rat house. One group of hunters who were canoeing through the rice spotted Toby's realistic spread and eased into shooting position thinking they had stumbled upon a sure thing. Toby ended the story by saying the two would be duck hunters nearly fell out of their canoe when the muskrat house warned them not to shoot the decoys!

Toby's favorite method of bagging a limit was to "sneak up on a flock". And he was a master of the sneak and stalk method. I learned much from his teachings on the subject. It mattered not how little natural concealment existed along a lakeshore or the bank of some marshy stream, Toby somehow nearly always made a silent, successful stalk.

But waterfowl weren't the only feathered game he could hit on the fly. Besides dad and his buddies going on their annual opening weekend duck hunt, for many falls an annual grouse and woodcock hunt also took place. With loaded vehicles, dad's gang would head deep into the Nicolet National Forest with hunting and camping gear and comb the thickets for ruffed grouse and "timberdoodles". Toby was also usually "top gun" when it came to harvesting those feathered rockets!

One of the most remarkable feats of wing shooting I ever witnessed occurred while on a hunt for sharp tailed grouse one gorgeous October afternoon. Dad, Toby and I, plus Old Pat and Toby's Springer spaniel were combing a grass-covered ravine looking for the resident flock of "sharpies". Toby crested a small knoll and flushed five birds. Fortunately for Toby, the birds did not all flush at the same time, but took off in a staggered take off pattern. But all five birds flushed in different directions! The eagle-eyed gunner emptied his old Browning with five well-aimed shots and all five sharp tails tumbled cleanly to earth! It was a spectacular show!

Another rare spectacle I recall occurred at Devine Lake. Toby and Charlie Goodyear were blinded up on the east shore in a dense patch of cattails. About a hundred yards further down the shoreline were dad and I. A small flock of four ringbills came whistling down the shoreline at mach two. Three quick shots sounded from our friend's blind, all of which were from Toby's Browning, and three dead ringbills lay twitching on the water. The lone bird kept on course and dad plucked it from the air with one shot. I'll never forget Toby's loud summation of the event!

"That's the end of that flock!"

To have known the man was indeed an honor! To have hunted with him and benefited from his vast knowledge of the sport represented something of such value no amount of money could have purchased it!

And so, if there are indeed ducks to hunt in heaven, I hope the person in charge put Toby next to a good marsh. He was a man who richly deserved it!

The Blizzard and The Mallard of '56

After graduation from Eagle River High School in May of 1955, a major decision needed to be made that surely would dramatically alter the course of my future. I needed to choose a college.

Due to what is commonly referred to as "a shortage of cash", narrowed my field of choice to three institutions of higher learning. Illinois Normal, Stevens Point State College, and Superior State College were selected as the "finalists".

After doing a minimal amount of research and a considerable amount of soul searching I selected Superior. Besides having a tuition I could afford, there were but two other major reasons for choosing Superior. One: It was the only state college in the Wisconsin system (except the U of Wisconsin in Madison) to have a hockey team. Two: The area around Superior was saturated with great places to hunt ducks.

As the summer of '55 flitted by, several additional close friends and buddies likewise chose Superior as their destination for the fall semester. Perhaps the fact that they, like me, played hockey and hunted ducks contributed more than a small part in their decisions.

A few days after Labor Day, Tom Dean, Doug Dean, Gene Olson and myself loaded our meager belonging in two vehicles and headed northwest to begin a new phase of our lives. Among our baggage were four shotguns and my duck skiff, which had been a Christmas present to me from Uncle Bud a number of years earlier.

****

Our first year together at Superior State was fantastic. All four of us made the varsity hockey team and we discovered a treasure trove of duck hunting beyond anything we had experienced back in our hometown area. Understandably, our grades suffered slightly from the "extra-curricular" activity during October and November, but we did well enough to wind up becoming sophomores by year's end.

But at the time, what seemed to be of vastly more importance to us, was the discovery of additional areas where we could hunt ducks during our second year of higher education.

One of our favorite haunts, due to the fact it was within five miles of our dormitory, was Allouez Bay. Located just outside the city limits, the one hundred-acre plus bay was thickly filled with wild rice. All we had to do was post standers along the shoreline and then have one of us head out into the rice with my duck skiff and flush the feeding birds. The skiff hunter always got some great jump shooting and the boys on the bank generally got in some close range pass shooting.

Frequently our morning or afternoon classes contained several empty seats during the duck season.

Ranging further east and south from the city of Superior we continued to locate pot holes, small secluded lakes, and streams that held good populations of ducks, but for whatever reason had few duck hunters! What more could one ask for? By the fall of 1956 we were much better prepared!

During the summer of '56 the Dean Boys and I located an ancient Old Town cedar strip canoe, which the owner of had deemed was ready for the dump. We claimed salvage rights, removed the rotting canvas, and with Uncle Bud's expertise covered the hull with a layer of fiberglass. Other than adding about another hundred pounds to the seventeen-foot craft, we now had a real jump-shooting vessel. I managed to add a side mount near the stern, which would hold my little three-horse power Johnson outboard, and we were all set for the duck season of '56!

To save additional funds, which for all of us were still in short supply, we opted out of the dormitories and rented small housekeeping apartments. Tom and I found a tiny basement apartment owned by a Methodist Minister and his wife. We had our own kitchen and bath, with a couch that extended into a double bed. By squeezing in a small cot, we solved the sleeping arrangement.

Doug and Gene located in different apartments with some of our fraternity brothers and we were all set to tackle whatever the professors tossed at us. Then came duck season.

The previous season we had discovered a marshy, twisting stream about twenty miles south and east of Superior, named Bear Creek. Being of a devious nature, as are most duck hunters, we developed code names for all our favorite hunting spots so as to not let other nimrods discover where we were shooting all our ducks. Along the banks of Bear Creek someone had posted their property with "No Trespassing" signs that also included a warning which proclaimed, "Danger, Dynamite". And so, Bear Creek became Dynamite Creek. And for hunters, who like jump shooting, our name indicated the quantity and quality of hunting we discovered!

October zipped by all too rapidly, and although our rented box at the local refrigeration plant contained many duck dinners, still the northern flights continued to deposit new comers into our favorite hunting spots well into November. It was just a little over a week before deer season when the "Mother of All Blizzards" struck.

For several days prior to the appearance of the giant storm, thousands of ducks, geese and other assorted waterfowl rafted up on the bay between Barker Island and the mainland of Lake Superior in the city limits of the community of Superior. Doug, Tom and I had spectacular shooting in Allouez Bay and Amnicon Lake. Little did we suspect why there was such a huge influx of migrating birds. On Thursday of that week Doug and I discovered why, and we quite possibly had a close brush with the Grim Reaper!

Tom and I were awakened shortly before six a.m. by a furious pounding on our apartment door. I, being closest to the noise, crawled out of bed and opened it to find Doug standing there dressed in his duck hunting garb and hip boots. His cap and shoulders were covered with fresh snow, and his face contained a grin a mile wide.

"Man is it snowing out!", was his opening remark. And even though I was still half-asleep, I had already figured that out.

"Let's cut our morning classes and go duck hunting! They ought to be flying like hell in this storm!"

I was suddenly wide-awake, as was Tom, my roommate. I immediately accepted Doug's offer, but Tom reluctantly declined, announcing he was scheduled to take a major exam in one of his morning classes and didn't dare miss it. In a matter of minutes I was dressed and Doug and I were heading south on highway 53 in his 1950 Ford Sedan.

We launched our canoe at the public boat launch on Amnicon Lake and fought a fierce southwest gale to reach our blind on the south tip of the island. Snow was falling in massive sheets and soon our decoys looked like a flock of sea gulls. Nary a duck did we see. After two hours of watching a snow filled sky, we picked up our decoys, returned to the boat launch, with intentions to return to Superior. But Doug suggested what he envisioned as, "another short hunt".

Seeing as though we were only a few miles from Dynamite Creek, maybe we should paddle upstream a couple of miles and kill some mallards. After all, that would be a great place for a flock or two of stupid Canadian Greenheads to be riding out the storm. We convinced each other our hunch was correct.

By the time we launched our canoe where Bear Creek crossed Highway A, the snow had accumulated to a depth over a half foot and was still falling steadily. We hesitated slightly, beginning to worry about getting back to Superior if the snow continued, but surmised the county snowplow trucks would have the roads plowed soon.

We flipped a coin to see who would sit in the front seat and be the first shooter. It was our custom to take turns as shooters, with each of us getting one chance to bag any ducks that jumped in range, and then switching places to give the one who had been in the rear paddling the front seat. I won the toss.

A quarter mile of empty water slipped by. Then another quarter mile disappeared behind us. Not one duck did we encounter. However, the snowfall had increased noticeably and the wind had begun to shift to the northwest. And although the surface of the creek was not beginning to freeze, the amount of falling snow was beginning to form into a thick layer of slush on the surface.

We stopped to pow-wow. It was decided to go just a little further and then turn back. We finally began to suspect all the ducks had been able to forecast the storm and headed south ahead of it. (It was a few years later before I realized ducks, as well as many other wild species of wild game, were more often than not smarter than humans!)

About two bends further upstream we spotted a trail in the slush that looked like a muskrat or a small beaver had crossed the creek. But then, to our surprise, from under the overhanging speckled alders up jumped a hen mallard. My shotgun was raised with numb hands and the lone mallard's migration ended.

Doug made a comment to the effect that at least we weren't skunked. Then we turned the canoe around and headed back downstream towards our car. I unloaded my gun and put it in my soaked case, and began to help my companion paddle.

We soon realized we were in trouble! The amount of slush was becoming so thick and heavy our canoe no longer glided forward with every stroke. It was like trying to move a canoe across a bowl of gooey pancake dough! The temperature was beginning a noticeable downward slide and our wet gloves were beginning to freeze. We stopped and took off our hip boots, removed one layer of wool socks, and put them on our hands to help ward off the cold.

By the time we reached Doug's car, we were nearly exhausted. It was now mid afternoon, and the snow was still showing no sign of letting up. Upon loading our canoe on the car tops and securing it, more trouble reared its ugly head. Now with more than a foot of snow on the ground, and the fact the highway still had not been plowed, all the Ford could do was spin it's wheels. We were stuck in a blizzard!

The snow-covered surface of Highway A showed no sign that any vehicles had passed since we had arrived at Bear Creek some four hours earlier. There was nothing else to do but start hiking towards civilization. And the nearest dwelling was a small tavern about a mile and a half further north near Amnicon Lake. Shouldering our cased shotguns, we pulled down the bills of our caps and headed into the teeth of the howling blizzard.

Dusk was settling in by the time we had fought our way through drifts and swirling snow to the sanctuary of the Amnicon Bar and Grill. Surprisingly, the bar was open, although empty of customers. The owner knew us, as his establishment was a regular stop for numerous college kids who were in need of some liquid refreshment. At the time, Wisconsin allowed eighteen-year-olds to buy and consume beer from taverns that sold only beer and wine.

After wolfing down two super sized hamburgers and a double order of fries, all washed down with several bottles of what made Milwaukee famous, Doug and I continued to ponder our fate.

The owner of the bar informed us he had heard a news broadcast on his radio that the county had decided to pull all their snowplows off the roads until the storm abated. The nearest plowed highway was another three and a half miles further north at a crossroads called Four Corners.

We used his phone to call my roommate, Tom, and asked if he could find someone to drive to Four Corners and pick us up. We guessed we could make the trip on foot in a little over an hour. Tom agreed to try, but could give us no reassuring positive answer.

Trusting the tavern owner to be the keeper of two shotguns, one Winchester Model 12 pump and one Remington Wingmaster 870, we once again headed out and into the brutal storm and headed north to hopefully rendezvous with,......someone!

The warm interior of the bar, plus the several bottles of beer we consumed had made us over confidant in our ability to combat Mother Nature in her own element. Without benefit of flashlights, we felt our way through the nearly pitch-dark night, traveling head on into what seemed like an unrelenting gale force wind. Our eyes watered continuously causing our tears to freeze solid, and the wind driven snowflakes stung the exposed skin on our faces like driven sand. We encountered snowdrifts that were waist deep. Snow worked its way into our hip boots and melted, soaking our pants and adding to the pace at which our body heat was sucked away by the icy blasts of Old Man Winter.

I actually remember very little detail of the two and half-hours it took us to transverse the three and a half miles to Four Corners. To our relief, there was Tom with another of our friends who had volunteered to use his brand new 1957 Thunderbird to come to our rescue!

Finally back in our apartment, I filled the bathtub with hot water and soaked my chilled body for nearly an hour. Then I slept for ten hours.

By morning the storm had subsided to a few scattered snowflakes which were still being pounded to earth by a vicious northwest gale. When our last afternoon class ended, Doug, Tom and I were given a ride to Bear Creek to retrieve Doug's car. The county snowplows had nearly buried it with snow, which required us to shovel for over an hour to free it from its frozen prison.

My mallard was frozen stiff, and resided in the kitchen sink of our apartment for another day until it was thawed enough to clean. I marked the package with a special notation, in order to be sure I would know it was the "Mallard in a Blizzard" when we cooked it.

And later that winter when Tom, Doug and I dined on the roasted beauty, I said the prayer. And I gave heartfelt thanks that Doug and I had survived to celebrate our survival in "The November Blizzard of '56"!

Manitoba Moments

My dad often promised to take me to special places for purposes of hunting, fishing, camping, or all of the above. And I can't remember a promise he didn't keep. Sometimes the timing had to be postponed, because as often happened a minor detail about "making a living" would delay our departure. They don't make people any better than my dad was.

Realizing my love of waterfowling exceeded his, although not by much, we talked often about taking a trip to Canada "someday" to find out what real duck hunting was all about. And "someday" occurred in October of 1958.

In May of that same year I had dragged my fiance down the aisle and we exchanged vows. I still had a full year of college ahead of me, and money was still as scarce as hen's teeth, so our honeymoon consisted of a three day, two-night tour of Michigan's western Upper Peninsula.

At the beginning of the fall term of my senior year, my new bride's acceptance of the news that I would be leaving college, and her, for a week in early October was met with less than an enthusiastic response. And despite the fact that I had reminded her well before our marriage I was a hunting and fishing maniac, and had a different set of priorities than she, well,...... let the point rest by my saying "Peggy was not a happy camper."

But, the trip went off as planned, and my bride was still living in our apartment waiting for my return. And now that an additional forty-six years have evaporated, she's still with me.

During that forty-six years, Peggy's attitude has improved vastly. Now when I plan an extended hunting trip, she asks how long I'll be gone,......and then adds, "Take your time honey!" I like to think I've trained her well!

****

The planned pilgrimage to the Promised Land of Endless Ducks included four duck hunting devotees. Besides yours truly, the Best Man at my wedding, Doug Dean signed on. The second pair of hunters was my dad, Andy Anderson and one of his buddies, Charlie Goodyear.

My 1953 Chevy Sedan was selected as the vehicle, which would deliver us into paradise. Doug and I strapped our Old Town canoe onto a small boat trailer, and all our gear was stowed inside. Then we used a canvas tarp to secure the load and keep it dry in case we hit rain or snow on the two day trip to Manitoba. Charlie also had an Old Town canoe, and his was secured to my car tops.

Dad and Charlie drove to Superior to meet Doug and I, then early the next morning the four of us, looking perhaps a bit like the Beverly Hillbilly's, headed north and west for a new adventure.

Our destination was Portage la Prairie, a small city set in an expanse of open prairie a few miles south of Lake Manitoba. We were smack dab in the center of one of Canada's greatest duck factories!

The late 50's were drought years, and water levels were low, as had been the spring hatch of ducks. Or so said the local duck "xpurts". Undaunted by this prediction we purchased our licenses and bought a case of number 5 heavy duck loads at the local sporting goods store, then headed towards the vast marshlands a few miles north.

Our first afternoon was drenched with disappointment. The area where we had been directed to hunt was devoid of water and likewise ducks. We did succeed in getting some pass shooting at ducks coming and going from the main body of water further north, to the multitude of grain fields south and west.

How well I remember folding up the first duck that passed over the clump of marsh grass in which I was hiding. Thinking it was a young hen mallard, at first I was mystified by it's huge, flat bill. Then I realized I had bagged my first shoveler. It was the only duck I bagged that sunny afternoon. My partners added several additional birds, as few ducks did we see. But one afternoon does not a duck hunt make!

Back in town at our motel we made our pessimism known to the proprietor. He suggested we contact one of the local guides, Pete Johnson, who would show us plenty of targets to shoot at. We discussed the option, took stock of our meager financial situation, and drove to Pete's residence.

Pete was a Native American, a Cree, he informed us. Pete lost no time in busting the stereotype mold I had formed in my mind concerning Native Americans, which I had acquired by watching numerous grade B western movies as a sub-teenager. You may remember the Hopalong Cassidy, Tom Mix, Randolph Scott, the Lone Ranger, and a host of other good guys with white hats that generally made most Indians the bad guys. Few Indians had any speaking parts and if they did, it was something like, "Ugg, white man speak with forked tongue.", or some other foolish jibberish.

Pete was very articulate, spoke with a British accent, and had an air about him that told you he knew his business. We all took an instant liking to Pete and hired him to show us some real duck hunting. His smile somehow translated into an unspoken answer that assured us he'd give us our monies worth.

Pete instructed us to pick him up at his house the following morning at four a.m., then added, "Pack a lunch." His daily fee was $40.00, half days for $25.00. We signed up for a half-day.

In the blackness of pre-dawn, Pete sat in the passenger seat of my Chevy and directed our travel to a rustic launch site on the banks of a large river. We unloaded our gear, loaded it into our two canoes and began paddling northward in the inky darkness. Millions of stars twinkled overhead, supplying us with a meager light source. Within a few minutes of paddling against a brisk northwest wind produced labored breathing, which created small clouds of frozen water vapor around our faces each time we exhaled. It was chilly!

After fifteen to twenty minutes of paddling, our guide seated comfortably in the center of our canoe directed us to a trail on the east side of the riverbank. It was, as Pete informed us, "A short portage trail to his huntin' spot".

"Short" meant about four hundred yards of frozen mud. First our bags of decoys, guns and lunch made the crossing. The second trip was with our canoes. Now we were really sweating! Once our canoes were reloaded, more paddling continued, which at least kept our bodies warm.

Finally, after what seemed like several hours, (actually probably another twenty minutes) Pete called a halt at a small grassy island. He instructed dad and Charlie to put out their decoys and blind up in the tall marsh grass that covered the island.

Then off we went again! Another fifteen or twenty minutes later we finally stopped again. We came ashore on what we later realized was a fairly large grass covered frozen mud flat, on the south shore of Lake Manitoba. As the eastern horizon slowly eased to pink, orange and yellow, we put out our three dozen assorted decoys, threw together a makeshift blind from clumps of tall marsh grass, and waited.

Well before legal shooting time the sound that even sends goose bumps up the arms of a seasoned veteran of the marsh reached our ears. The distinct whistle of wind rushing over feathered wings overhead! Knowing from many past experiences that we wouldn't be able to see the early morning risers, we looked skyward anyway. Our only reward was an awareness of a quickening of our pulse.

As morning slowly beat back the blackness of night we began to see what at first looked like rapidly moving black clouds silhouetted against the blushing eastern horizon. But clouds they were not! Ducks! Huge flocks of ducks were in constant motion, shaking the water from their feathers in an age-old early morning ritual! Doug and I gazed at a spectacle that we had previously only read about! Now, nearly fifty years later I still class that memory as "awesome"!

Once shooting time arrived we didn't have long to wait for what we had driven over five hundred miles to do. A small flock of mallards left a pair of their numbers upside down in our decoys. Then I bagged a drake canvasback that came screaming downwind, being pushed to full velocity. Next came teal, then gadwalls, bluebills and ringbills. The canvasback really excited me, as it was the first of its kind that I had ever bagged. Or ever shot at for that matter.

Before an hour was up Doug and I had witnessed more ducks than we generally saw in an entire season back in northern Wisconsin! Indeed, we were in a duck hunter's heaven!

As the morning progressed, Pete left me to guard our decoy spread and paddled Doug to a distant island where we had spotted some Canadian honkers set down. The pair was successful in sneaking close enough to bag one of the giant birds.

Upon the return of my partners, I directed them to a dead bird I had bagged during their absence, which had floated downwind and hung up on a clump of weeds. I had no idea what species it was, as it did not resemble any which was familiar to me.

When my two retrievers pulled our canoe back ashore I asked our guide what kind of duck I had downed. I'll never forget the reply! Pete, a Cree Indian, replied in a perfect English accent, "I say old chap, you killed a bloody Rudy Duck"! It, like the canvasback I had shot earlier in the day, was the first of its kind I had ever bagged.

By shortly before eleven a.m. Doug and I had secured our legal limits. Throughout the morning we had been able to hear a fairly steady salvo of shotgun blasts from the direction where dad and Charlie were blinded up. We picked up our decoys and paddled to the grassy island, which Pete had selected for their morning hunt.

Upon our arrival we discovered our companions sitting on the shore, smiling. Dad was puffing on a cigarette and Charlie had fired up one of his five cent Lord Clinton cigars. I assumed they too had limited out. I was correct in my assumption.

By the time we dropped Pete off at his home in Portage la Prairie it was well after three p.m. We asked him what we owed him, and he replied "Twenty-Five dollars,.....American. That's what we agreed upon yesterday."

Dad looked at his watch and then at his three hunting buddies, then back to Pete. "But we kept you out way past noon. We should give you more than a half-day's wages". Pete shook his head in a negative response.

Dad turned to his partners and whispered, "Each of you give me ten bucks."

Pete accepted the "tip", plus also accepted a half dozen of the forty ducks we had bagged. Any way you looked at it, we still came out way on top!

We spent the morning hours of the next two days hunting the area Pete had so generously and professionally guided us to. The only thing that changed, besides not having Pete around to entertain us with his English wit and wisdom, was the weather. The cold snap in which we had hunted on our second day in Manitoba quickly vanished and was replaced by sun-drenched skies and gentle southwest breezes.

I do recall lying back on the grass-covered mud flat, and bagging several drake pintails as they passed overhead. Like the canvasback and the Rudy duck, they too were my first of the species!

After finishing dinner on the fourth day, dad called for a meeting. It was agreed we'd need to leave our newfound paradise a day early. Temperatures had risen to a point, which threatened to cause our ducks to begin spoiling. There was no refrigeration available for hunters, and our birds were hanging in an old shed behind the motel.

Before daylight the following morning we packed seventy-six ducks and a goose into the trunk of my Chevy, and headed south. The homeward trek was reasonably uneventful, except for a memorable experience at the International Border.

The Customs Agent asked the usual questions, including, "What do you have to declare?"

Having filled out a sheet of paper in advance, listing each specie of waterfowl that was packed in our trunk and the exact number of each, dad answered, "Seventy six ducks and one goose". (Which was still twenty-four ducks short of our combined legal possession limits)

The agent never blinked an eye nor looked up. He filled in the data in a routine manner. We looked at each other slightly surprised, as we expected to be checked, duck by duck. The trunk of my Chevy was so crammed with birds that wing tips, feet and bills protruded from the edges of my trunk cover!

Relieved at not having to unpack all our ducks for a body count, which I'm sure would have been time consuming, we prepared to depart the interior of the customs office. Just then another car containing four hunters and bearing Minnesota license plates pulled into the checkpoint and stopped.

As we were leaving, we overheard the same questions asked of the new arrivals. When the leader of the group answered the question, "What do you have to declare?", with an answer of, "Six ducks.", The custom agent looked up suspiciously and said while pointing, "Pull your vehicle right over there."

As we drove away a small army of custom agents were in the process of what looked like dismantling the vehicle in question. We often wondered why or what made the custom agent suspicious. Dad said it was because the group was from Minnesota. But then again, Dad was a Packer fan.

The day following our arrival back in Superior, dad and Charlie said their good-byes and left. But each of them only took ten ducks. That left Doug and I with fifty-six ducks and a goose to clean, package and store in our rented freezer at the local locker plant. The two of us spent an entire day parked in a deserted field well outside of town picking ducks and listening to the New York Yankees defeat our beloved Milwaukee Braves in the final game of the 1958 World Series.

But what to hell, baseball is only a game. Duck hunting is serious business!

A Father's Farewell

Fifty-two years of age is way too young for a person to die. Especially the very good. And my dad was an exceptional human being. I knew of no individual who ever felt any animosity or ill will towards dad. He was kind of heart with a totally jolly disposition and rarely complained about life's frequent tough blows.

He lost his mother when he was eight; his father passed away eight years later. The youngest of five brothers and one sister, dad inherited the family farm just in time to be slapped by the Great Depression. In 1932 the bank foreclosed and dad lost his farm.

At age 23 he was now homeless. A person of lesser inner strength may not have survived three such crushing blows at such an early age. But dad was not a quitter. His optimism and love of life drove him forward and allowed him to start a new life in Wisconsin's Northwood's.

He married his childhood sweetheart in 1935 and a son was born to the couple in 1937.

Dad was an amazing man. During his lifetime he had been a farmer, worked in his dad's lumber camps, tended bar, drove delivery trucks, ran a gas station, built and managed a resort, owned his own sawmill, became a legendary fishing guide, and owned a grocery store and service station.

For nearly all his life the wolf seems to be lurking just outside his door. The struggle to rise above adversity was a long and drawn out affair.. But finally he and mom achieved that goal. The final six years of his life offered a reasonable amount of financial stability that allowed them to lead a relaxed life style.

Having never really been sick a day in his entire life, a sudden and fatal heart attack took him away on December 29, 1961. It just wasn't fair! But dad had often told me that often life isn't fair. Once again he was right!

****

Peggy and I, plus our two toddlers, were spending our second school term in central Florida. I was totally enjoying my teaching career, my wife was a stay at home mom, and my parents lived but a few blocks away enjoying the fruits of their new business. Life was good!

Dad and mom bought a small grocery store and service station a few miles north of Orlando in the late '50's. The two of them were able to manage the business with a minimum of extra help, and my folks were enjoying the warm winters and the new friends they had collected in the sunny south. In May they would return to Wisconsin and run the small resort the two of them had hacked out of the wilderness until after Labor Day. During their absence a retired couple who lived in a trailer court just behind "Anderson's Delicatessen and Service Station" ran the business. The arrangement and new life style was working out wonderfully!

Christmas of 1961 arrived, allowing Grandma and Grandpa Anderson to spend the day with their son, daughter in law and the two grandkids. After an early Christmas dinner, I talked dad into going duck hunting with me to the swish grass marshes of the St. Johns River. Having had little time in recent years to do some duck hunting he eagerly agreed.

By two thirty we were silently exploring the many twisting channels provided by the St. Johns between Lake Monroe and Lake Jessup. It was a gorgeous afternoon! A bright deep blue cloudless sky stretched overhead which drove temperatures into the mid 70's. I paddled from the rear seat of my canoe and dad sat in the front with his Wingmaster at ready.

The day was way too nice for ducks, but as always there were a few scattered throughout the marshy grassland through which the river flowed. Numerous small minor channels interconnected small ponds on which many varieties of waterfowl and marsh birds thrived.

Turkey buzzards rode the wind currents high above us, slightly resembling the majestic bald eagles dad and I so often saw back in Wisconsin. We came upon great blue herons, snow-white egrets, soft-shelled turtles, and a multitude of various songbirds. The range cattle were content to chew their cuds and watch us silently glide by.

There was hushed conversation between father and son. Conversations of hunts past, and plans for hunts in the future. The afternoon provided me with a treasured memory, which turned out to be the last one my dad could provide.

Dad got in enough shooting to make any day in the marsh a success, although neither of us has ever measured our enjoyment by how much of anything we harvested. For dad and I it was always just "The Going and Being There".

By five thirty we were back at the landing. Our bag included two mottled mallards, (a sub-species of mallard that live only in the Gulf States), two ringbills, one blue winged teal and a drake hooded merganser.

Two days later we dined like kings on the fruits of our labors. Two days later dad was dead.

I worked at mom and dad's store that fateful evening, pumping gas and cleaning dead bugs from many windshields. Normal closing time was eight p.m. About seven thirty dad asked if I minded closing up for him, as he had developed a slight headache and was going to take a couple of aspirins and go to bed. I told him that would be no problem and promptly locked up and said good night to mom at eight sharp.

An hour later there was a knock on our door. A gentleman who lived in the trailer park behind my folk's store told me my father was very ill and I should go to my parent's living quarters at once.

I arrived back at the store a few minutes later and discovered a tragedy. Dad was dead, mom in tears.

A doctor arrived shortly and informed us there was nothing he could do. His opinion was that dad's aorta had burst. Death, he said, had probably been almost instantaneous.

Although that tragic night occurred over forty years ago, I still haven't completely gotten over the blow. There had been so many things we had planned to do together, so many things we wanted to do. It just didn't seem fair.

But life for the living goes on. And all that knew him are much richer for the experience. Thanks dad, for all you did for me and all the wonderful things you taught me about life and living. You were one hell of a teacher!

Duke

    I've always been, and undoubtedly always will be, a dog lover. My first recollections of interacting with dogs are but bits and pieces that remain hidden in the deep recesses of my tiny childhood memory banks.

    When I was but knee high to a toadstool, we had two mutt dogs, the "Heinz 57" varieties, named Chum and Jip. When I was about two or three, Chum, who actually was a bum, wandered off one day and never returned. Dad and Uncle Bud figured a wolf probably had him for lunch. Jip was a deer chaser, and that's not a good thing. One fall afternoon when Uncle Ed was hunting deer, he caught Jip in the act and shot the deer chaser. I wasn't happy about loosing our dog, but Uncle Ed did the right thing. If you've ever seen what dogs do to deer they catch, you'd understand.

Then came Pat, a curly haired black cocker spaniel. I think dad bought Pat when I was about four or five. He soon became my best pal and playmate, but fell victim to a hit and run driver from Illinois when I was six.

Grandma Jorgensen and I were harvesting blueberries along the roadside of the county highway that passed near our homestead. Pat took chase after a chipmunk, which darted across the highway to safety, but my dog got run over by some tourist driving a new Buick. He never even slowed up after running poor Pat over.

Pat lived for a few minutes, with blood pouring out of his nose and mouth, and died as I cradled him in my arms. Uncle Bud dug a hole by the side of the road and my family and I held a short funeral service. I cried for several days.

Then dad went right out and bought another black cocker spaniel, just like Pat. And guess what? We named him Pat. He was with us for fourteen years and eventually became known as "Old Pat". But you've already heard about Old Pat in my earlier tales.

After Old Pat disappeared in 1955, I remained dogless for the next eight years. With college to finish, a marriage, and then the two kids that showed up, plus earning a living, somehow I just didn't seem to have time to include another dog in my life.

While I attended college, dad and mom migrated to Florida for the winter seasons and loved it so much they talked Peggy and I into coming south after I graduated and join them. This we did in January of 1960.

I landed a teaching job at a Junior High School in Orlando, and taught there for seven school terms. Although I returned to my true home in Wisconsin each summer to work around the family resort and guide anglers.

By 1963 Peggy and I decided the time was right to get another dog. One who would be a great family member, love kids, and retrieve ducks. And along came Duke!

****

We paid fifty dollars for Duke, which was a ton of money for a teacher making $3600.00 a year and $25.00 a day during the summer guiding fisherperson. But he was one of the best bargains I ever spent money on!

As I recall there were about eight or ten rolly polly Black Labrador pups in the litter. Peggy and I decided on one of the bigger males. And as it turned out, Duke kept getting bigger and bigger until he was real big. One hundred and ten pounds big!

Duke had a head on him like a Kodiak Brown Bear, well filled with intelligence. Like nearly all Labs, he was friendly and loving, unless someone appeared to be threatening a family member. Also, nobody, and I mean nobody but family members could enter our home or our car unless we told Duke it was "O.K.". And that's a good thing!

We bought Duke in July of '63 and made a place for him in the rear of our station wagon when we headed back to Florida for the school term. He behaved much better than our two youngsters, Chris and Cherie. Duke loved to go for a car ride. During our frequent stops on the route between Northern Wisconsin and Central Florida, there were many stops for ice cream cones. The clerks who dished up the cones often looked confused when four persons ordered five cones. Duke also loved ice cream!

At the age of twelve weeks he made his first of what eventually became hundreds of retrieves. Still a small, waddling puppy, I took Duke along with me on the opening day of dove season, which happened sometime in late September. I dropped a bird into a tangled thicket of palmetto bushes and spent ten or fifteen fruitless minutes searching for the crippled dove. Returning to my makeshift blind, upset over my inability to be a retriever, I realized Duke was missing. I began calling frantically, as I was hunting an open field at the edge of a dismal, snake infested swamp.

Near the panic stage, I started running towards the area where I had been looking for my downed bird, guessing Duke had followed me there and disappeared into the palmetto thicket. Just before I reached my destination little Duke emerged from the thicket with a small bundle of feathers in his mouth. He had found my dove!

There have been few times in my life when I may have experienced an emotional high larger than I received at that moment. Several thoughts sped through my mind in rapid succession. My dog isn't lost or bitten by a rattlesnake! Ain't he cute waddling towards me with his first retrieve! And,.....Man oh man, is this dog going to be a great retriever! And for the next nine seasons he was!

As the pages of the calendar flitted by one by one during that wonderful hunting season of '63, Duke found and retrieved quail, as well as more doves. Duck season rolled around in late November and the hours and hours of time spent on training sessions paid big dividends.

My main duck hunting grounds were along the marshes and flooded backwater sloughs along the famed St. Johns River that snakes its way north through central Florida. Back in the 60's there were gobs of ducks, dozens of hot spots to hunt, and virtually no duck hunters! And duck season extend through Christmas Vacation, giving me two full weeks to get serious about my favorite sport.

Through the six duck seasons I hunted central and east Florida, I found my general success rates much better than in my native northern Wisconsin, and on a par with numerous other regions I have hunted in, including Canada and the western prairie pothole country. And during the three seasons Duke shared a blind with me, or with myself and several friends I converted to being duck hunters, Duke developed into a genuine blue ribbon retriever!

Duke, like all the Labs that have followed, was trained to sit outside the blind and always be "ready for action". I know this is contrary to most "traditional" training philosophies, but, "That's the way I like it,...Uh Huh."

First off, a good retriever will often spot incoming birds well before the hunter does. And you'll soon get the unspoken message by watching your dog's body language. And the dog is always looking in the direction of the incoming birds. Often during the early morning low light period, your dog can be like having a personal radar unit. Their hearing is much better than that of a human, and your dog will hear approaching waterfowl well before you will. You'll soon learn that keeping an eye on your radar set will result in getting more ducks. Or at least more shots at ducks!

Second: When a bird falls, a dog outside the blind will see exactly where it falls. And in the case of multiple falling birds, that's a real lifesaver if you are hunting heavy cover, such as wild rice, marsh grass, or hyacinth plants in the south.

Third: If a bird is winged, or crippled, a dog outside the blind will be off and running, (or swimming) after the cripple rather that sitting obediently by Mr. Owner, waiting for him to give the "fetch" command. Dad often told me, "Keep your mouth shut and let the dog hunt. They know a hell of a lot more about how to find a bird than you do." And you know dad was right!

Four: This is just a personal feeling from someone that loves and respects "man's best friend". Let your faithful retriever be in a position to always "be in on the action". From first sighting the birds to reaping the accolades and love pats when the bird is retrieved and dropped at your boots. Isn't he or she the most important part of the hunt? The dog certainly is on my duck hunting trips!

Duke and I shared many memorable outings while hunting together in some out of the way places throughout central Florida. Some memories conger up good feelings and some on the negative side.

Duke was bitten in the ear by a rattlesnake one Sunday afternoon as he was searching for a downed dove in a dense patch of weeds. Hopefully your dog will never require the services of a Vet on a Sunday afternoon. I nearly lost my friend before I was able to secure medical attention. We were lucky! The snake's fangs passed all the way through Duke's ear, so he only received a small dose of the poison.

A year later he contracted heartworms, and I nearly lost him again. But after months of shots and visits to the Dog Doctor, he fully recovered.

There was a third close call for both of us. Prior to 1966 B. D. (that's "Before Disney"), there was oodles of open range grazing land in central Florida. At the time, Florida was the number two, behind Texas, in the raising of beef cattle. Many areas along the St. Johns River were wide-open rangeland, with large herds of cattle roaming the grassy flood plain. This was also true of many low-lying areas near the shores of many of the huge lakes scattered along the stretch of the mighty St. Johns. Generally, a situation such as mixing cattle and duck hunters isn't a bad thing, unless the beef cattle are those horrible beasts from India, the ugly spirited Brahma species! And most of the beef cattle in Florida were Brahma and Brahma/Domestic cross breeds.

Duke and I found an untapped duck-hunting region along the north shore of Lake Monroe, just a few miles from Sanford, FL, which was chucked full of places to hunt ducks. But besides having a healthy population of ducks, it also had a healthy population of ornery Brahma beef cattle.

To reach this land of golden opportunity it was necessary to launch a small boat at a public launch on the north shore of Lake Monroe, then motor a mile or so up a small drainage canal to reach the area where the ducks and cattle were located. Generally, the cattle would move far across the field at the sight of a human carrying a sack of decoys and a large black dog.

Besides ducks and cattle, the wetlands were home to hundreds of coots. Duke and I had an established ritual once our morning hunt was finished and my decoys were back in the sack. Coots, not being the Albert Einstein of the waterfowl community, would not venture very far from a hunter, even if many shots were fired during a hunt. Coots would raft up in tight formations in the water filled depressions and just sit and eat. Duke loved chopped up cooked coot, and serving coot to my retriever cut down on the Purina Chow bill.

I'd load up my 12 gauge with number 8 field loads, (keeping in mind we've talking about the pre-steel shot era for waterfowl) send Duke to scare up the coots, and generally fill a limit of ten birds in short order.

But for some reason on this particular day in question, Duke decided to visit the cattle and bark at the bovine's babies! And he really raised the dander of the Daddy Brahmas!

A half dozen of the fire breathing hump backed monsters quickly put the run on the barking intruder, who with tail tucked between his legs lost no time in retreating to the what he hoped would be the safety of his master!

Duke envisioned a secure location would be just behind his master, looking between master's legs, while continuing to bark at the charging bulls,.....who were rapidly bearing down on the object of their hatred!

I swear, my life began to pass before my unbelieving eyes! Here we were, in the middle of a soggy, grass covered field, the nearest tree being over a half-mile distance, as was my boat! Before me, coming on full throttle was somewhere in the neighborhood of ten tons of horrible hoofs, horns and hide!

My initial reaction must have been pure instinct, as all I remember of that terrifying few moments was being petrified with fear. I dropped my sack of decoys, turned to face the charging herd and swallowed a lump in my throat the size of a basketball. When they were but ten yards from me I fired into the ground a few feet in front of their leader, spraying mud and water into his ugly, red eyed face.

To my utter surprise and momentary relief, the bulls came to a stop, not five yards from where I stood and trembled in my waders! (Surprisingly, that's all I did in my waders!) Duke continued to yip and yap, like some drunken lightweight boxer taunting Joe Lewis when he was in his prime. I yelled at him to "Shut Up", and reluctantly gave my friend a kick in the ribs. Duke decided to shut up.

Keeping my gun at ready with one hand, I picked up my sack of decoys and began a slow, but steady backward gait towards my distant boat. The bulls stood their ground for a few more seconds stomping their hooves, and then turned around and galloped back to the main herd.

I can't say how scared Duke might have been, but I can truthfully say never, and I mean NEVER, have I ever been that frightened.

After that experience every time Duke and I hunted what I named as "Brahmaville Marsh", we cancelled the coot hunt.

In early June of 1966 Peggy and I sold our home in Florida, packed up a U-Haul, and returned to my beloved north woods of Wisconsin. The announcement that Walt Disney was going to build a gigantic theme park near Orlando sent us packing "back up north". I predicted the peaceful southern setting that was pre-Disney would rapidly become a "zoo". Was I right?

Duke, like cheese, became better and better with age. He was methodical when it came to locating cripples. Rarely did any escape his ability to trail a wounded bird, or find a dead one buried deep within a cattail jungle. And when he was seven, he developed a startling new method of retrieving!

It was mid November. Many of the smaller lakes and duck holding potholes were frozen solid, but most of the creeks still had at least some stretches of semi-open water. Duke and I decided to check out Lost Creek on one Saturday afternoon after I had finished piling the last of our winter wood supply. Generally, the "crick" held some late migrating greenheads or black ducks, which often rested and fed during a break in their southern migration.

The first pool of open water was vacant. The second likewise. Trudging through a few hundred yards of a frozen black spruce and tamarack swamp lead us to bend number three. Faintly, through the screen of speckled alders that lined the bank of the stream I spotted a small flock of ducks. I glassed the migrants and discovered not mallards or blacks, but about a dozen plump, northern ringbills!

Dropping to my knees and whispering a command for Duke to "heal", together we inched our way into range. The leafy vegetation, such as marsh grass, fiddlehead ferns and alder leaves, had long since withered, died and fallen to the ground. Duke and I had little to mask our approach. But we did get nicely into range. As I raised to a kneeling position and readied my Wingmaster, the ringbills detected my movement and began taking off.

One nice thing about divers, they don't jump straight up like dabblers. They nearly always take off straight away from perceived danger, offering a "no brainer" shot. My first burst of number 6's dropped three out of the departing flock. And then, no doubt by another good dose of Devine Intervention, I scored twice more on shots two and three. I had my limit down with three shots!

Duke was already in the water by the time I pulled the trigger for the second time. But then he did something that I had never seen him, or any other retriever ever do! He reached the first bird, gently took it in his oversized mouth, but instead of turning to return the prize to master, Duke swam to the second bird, dropped the first one and took the second in his mouth. By now my bewilderment turned to giving a stern command. "Duke, bring the bird,..... now!"

Funny how I often forgot dad's suggestion that a good hunting dog is generally smarter than his master!

My command was met with indifference. Duke swam to duck number three, dropped number two and replaced it with number three. The pattern was repeated again with ducks number four and five.

By now I was leaning against a tamarack, wondering why my blue ribbon retriever had suddenly gone bonkers. But then I remembered something mom had said about Old Pat, and his streak of bullheadedness. "All males are bullheaded". Mom didn't tell lies either! Maybe Duke's compulsion to act bullheaded occasionally had now once again reared its ugly head.

After checking all five downed birds, Duke calmly swam to the one which was still twitching somewhat and professionally brought it back to Master, just like usual. He dropped the bird at my feet, looked me in the eye and,...so help me, he grinned!

Next, he turned around and leapt into the creek and swam to the four remaining birds. Taking one in his mouth he swam to the next one, took that one in his mouth also, and brought back two in one trip! For once in my life I was speechless! Dropping birds two and three on top of number one, he took one more swim and brought back the remained duo in his huge mouth!

Duke went on to do his "two in one trip" many times through the remainder of his hunting career, and once, he was successful in bringing in three bluebills in one trip! Once he tried for four, but lost one on the return trip!

When he was eight, my duck-hunting companion began having serious problems with his hips. The vet suspected he had been born with a minor case of hip displacia. It was time to purchase what would eventually become Duke's new replacement. We bought another black Lab. This time Peggy and I picked a small female and named her "Teal".

As well as I remember Duke's first retrieve of that crippled dove on his first hunt with me, I likewise remember his last. Important events generally become lasting memories.

It was opening day of the 1972 duck season. My son Chris and our oldest daughter Cherie occupied the family blind on Lost Creek, along with Duke and Teal. A flock of blue winged teal buzzed our decoys and when the shooting had ended four of their members lay scattered in our decoys.

Duke and Teal both headed out to finish the job. The water was shallow and muddy, making any retrieve from our blind rather difficult. Teal came ashore with ducks number one and two before a struggling Duke reached bird number three. Both Teal and Duke arrived back at the blind at about the same time, each carrying one of the final two ducks. Teal leaped ashore on her young, strong legs, but Duke simply stood in the muck and mire. He no longer had the ability to climb up and out of the creek.

I grabbed his collar and helped him up and into our blind. As always, he gently dropped his last retrieve at my feet, slowly walked out of the blind and lay down in a patch of dry ferns.

The following August we buried Duke on the crest of a small hill overlooking the yard of what had been his home. My four children erected a small cedar cross with a simple inscription:

Duke
1963 - 1973
You were our pal!

Alligator Alley

Before Peggy and I migrated to Florida in January of 1960, neither she nor I had ever ventured far from our respective home towns in northern Wisconsin. Peg had spent two summers in Montana with an aunt and uncle when she was in high school, and I had strayed as far as Chicago several times.

We had but isolated bits and pieces of information. ideas and concepts as to what "The South" was like. Movies generally portrayed the south as a place of beautiful mansions and "poo" folk. We knew Spanish Moss grew in most trees, after all both of us had seen Gone With The Wind a dozen or more times. But beyond that, a great mystery and many new experiences awaited us.

We received our first inklings of how different the south was going to be on our initial journey to the Sunshine State. Our third morning on the road found us stopping at a quaint cafe in Kentucky for breakfast. Among the items we ordered was a bowl of something we didn't order, but it looked like cream of wheat. The waitress informed us the mystery food was "grits", and a bowl came automatically with breakfast orders.

Peggy gave a spoonful to our infant son, who promptly made a ghoulish face and spit it out! I tasted it and agreed with our son's decision.

During a gas stop in Alabama the attendant smiled at me, and with his best Southern accent declared, "I'll bet yo'all 'ear from up nauth".

I smiled back, thinking he had looked at our license plate, and asked, "Yes we are. How did you guess?"

"Yo'all got mud grip treads on yer back tares".

I didn't have the heart to tell him they were Town and Country snow tires."

And let me tell you, there was a lot more for this north woods bumpkin to learn about the South in the weeks, months and years to come. But I guess I earned passing grades. There is nothing to take the place of "on the job training"!

Becoming accepted by the native "Florida Crackers", as they like to be called, was not an easy task. The Northern War of Aggression back in the 1860's had a lasting effect, which cast doubt on the honesty and inner character of all northern immigrants. After the Civil War the numerous sleazy northerner politicians who took advantage of the South's defeat were referred to as "Carpetbaggers". And although our modern luggage containers were now made of leather, nylon, or some other durable fabrics, suspicions as to our integrity was still suspect in the minds of many native southerners.

Against this background it was not surprising my early attempts to pump some information from the local nimrods about places to hunt and fish met with what I would best describe as "stony silence".

So, I had to do much of the footwork myself and spent a considerable amount of time on "wild goose chases" and making a fool out of myself. Although I've always found the later to be a fairly easy task.

We rented a small apartment from a wonderful middle aged couple named Jessup, in what was then a small, sleepy southern village a few miles north of Orlando. Longwood had a population of about three hundred middle class folks, the most of which were long time Florida residents. The Jessup's had two sons and two daughters, all of which were close in age to Peggy and I. It took me several months to convince the two sons, Frank and Jackie, that I was trustworthy enough to take along on a fishing trip on a remote stretch of the historic St. Johns River. And beside catching a nice mess of bass, I discovered DUCKS also lived there!

****

Most of my duck hunts during the first two seasons in Florida were spent along the sloughs and backwaters of the St. Johns. With the aid of some quadrangle maps I began exploring small lakes and "sink holes" that were off the beaten path. I found a treasure trove of great bass fishing water and several promising looking duck hunting marshes. I was feeling pretty smug that a northern transplant was finding his way around with a minimal amount of help.

One promising waterfowl slough was nestled in the midst of a Cyprus swamp about twenty miles north and east of Longwood. Once one left the paved highway, the slough was a mile drive on a sandy two rut dirt trail which wound through a forest of southern and yellow pine interspersed with Palmetto thickets. Driving those sandy back roads was almost like being in northern Wisconsin. Well, almost. The so called road skirted the edge of the Cyprus swamp, and a well worn game trail led me to a small, shallow three acre pond within the swamps interior.

The banks of the pond were covered with tall "swish grass", making it possible to blind up almost anywhere around the pond without actually making a blind. And there was no evidence that anyone else hunted there!

During the duck seasons of '62 and '63, I hunted the slough alone, which except when I'm with my dog is my favorite way to hunt. The slough treated me very well, but for reasons unknown to me only teal and an occasional small flock of ringbills frequented the secluded sanctuary. But little did I care, both species are fine table fare and challenging targets!

The remoteness of the slough was an extra added attraction. If the morning was devoid of ducks I could watch many varieties of songbirds flit back and forth from the marsh to the Cyprus swamp. In the pre-dawn darkness, after I had placed my decoys and settled into the comfort of the swish grass savoring a hot cup of coffee and something sweet, I could listen to owls hoot, crickets chirp, mosquitoes buzz, and what I assumed were giant bullfrogs croak. And most Florida sunrises are spectacular by anyone's standards! Ma Nature sure has created some wonderful sights and sounds!

When the 1964 duck season finally arrived, my new hunting companion was primed and ready. Duke and I enjoyed several mornings, in what in my mind had become my private little duck marsh.

Christmas vacation rolled around and I had two full weeks to practice doing what folks do on vacation. Becoming bored one warm afternoon when Peggy had our two kids over to grandma's house, Duke and I snuck off to our private pond to dissolve some boredom.

As duck hunting days go on a scale from one to ten, this particular afternoon was a minus six. No wind, high sky, but plenty of mosquitoes. I settled on putting out but one dozen decoys, as I actually expected this would be an outing when I'd return home with the same number of shells I left the house with. But one of the nicest things about doing stuff out of doors, there always seems to be lots of surprises when you often least expect them. Today was one of those "surprise days".

Less than fifteen minutes into our wait a pair of blue winged teal swept over my decoy spread. I pointed my Wingmaster at the lead bird and watched in awe as the second bird, a full six feet behind the leader, folded cleanly. Duke made a routine retrieve and received a small dog biscuit as his reward. I patted my friend on the head, told him what a wonderful guy he was and remarked, "At least we're not skunked".

A half-hour ticked away. Hardly a sound could be heard from any quarter. It seemed that all of Ma Nature's creatures were taking a mid afternoon nap. But then Duke and I heard the sound of jets.

But these jets were neither military nor commercial jets. These were rocket propelled feathered jets! A flock of thirty or more green winged teal where bearing down on the tiny pond, spiraling down from dizzy heights with cupped wings.

Tightly packed and without any hesitation, the entire flock roared over the decoy spread. I picked out a mature drake and fired. To my utter amazement, three teal crash-landed on the surface of the pond! Duke quickly sprang into action, as I stood dumbfounded with my jaw hanging down. On several occasions I had downed two birds with one shot, but never three!

However, my lucky shot created a major problem. Due to a low ebb in the continental duck population, the daily bag limit had been reduced to three ducks per day. Now I had four! As my retriever gleefully gathered up the third teal, his master was squirming on the painful horns of a dilemma.

Two sets of ethics, which were highly conflicting, began a battle in my mind.

One: Taking over a legal limit is unethical, as well as downright unsportsmanlike. And taking over a limit could also be expensive if a game warden were watching!

Two: My parents had instilled within me an age old concept which simply stated says; "Waste not, wont not"! As a youngster, food was never over plentiful, yet I never went hungry. To leave a precious resource to rot is waste in the worst sense! What was I going to do?

I took my time picking up my decoys, as my mind whirled attempting to reach a decision. When I finished putting the last decoy in my sack I still had not reached a decision. I kneeled down and began petting my dog, wishing I could ask for his opinion on what I should do. Then I looked up and there he was.

A man was standing at the edge of the Cyprus about thirty feet from my location. I did not know who he was, but the gray shirt with the shinny badge pinned on his chest told me what he was. A game warden!

Smiling, the officer walked towards me and offered a friendly greeting. I attempted unsuccessfully to swallow the large lump in my throat and somehow choked out a greeting in return.

The warden got right to the point.

"Been watchin' you since ya got here. I was doin' a little huntin' myself. I was sittin' in the grass over yonder and I guess ya didn't see me.", he explained, gesturing with his thumb across the small pond.

"No,.....I didn't see you. Hope I didn't spray you with my shot when I fired at those teal!" I shot a quick glance at the four teal laying in the grass next to my decoy bag, knowing full well he had already counted them. I swallowed another larger lump in my throat.

"No,..no, you didn't hit me. Your shot went high enough. But I'm glad ya didn't let 'um sit down and then bust 'um, or I'd got sprayed fer sure."

"It ain't any fun shooting them on the water.", was all I could think of to reply.

"Right smart bit of shootin' ya did."

"Thanks, but I guess maybe I shot just a tad too good."

He smiled again and took a good look at my four ducks. "That black dog of yers sure did a right nice job of retrievin'. Don't see many black Labs in these here parts. He's sure well behaved."

"Thanks. Yes, his name is Duke. He's a great dog. Never had a Lab before, but yes, he's good."

"May I see yer license?"

I reached inside my waders and struggled to remove my billfold from a rear pants pocket. With slightly trembling hand I removed the license and handed it to the warden.

"Everything looks o.k. Got yer signature in ink across the Federal Duck Stamp. Lot's of hunters forget to do that." With that he handed back my license.

The warden scratched his chin for a second and continued. "Now I know ya shot one duck over yer limit, and yer dog retrieved it. You accepted it, so that puts you in possession of it. If ya'd left the dang thing floatin' out there and walked away, you'd not be breakin' the law." He smiled again.

"Yes, I'm aware of that officer. But I'm sure my retriever isn't". I shot a faint smile back at the warden.

"I'm also aware that ya only shot one shell at that flock of teal, and there was no way ya could have planned to kill three ducks with one shot. I've bin around long enough to figure out if a guys violating or just had an accident. Ya had an accident."

"You're right. I'm usually lucky if I hit one bird."

"I watched ya shoot. I'm not so sure yer right about bein' just lucky".

"Thanks for the compliment. You caught me on one of my good days".

"Well, here's what I'm gonna do, young fella,......I'm gonna make believe I only see three ducks over there. I'll guess yer a guy who eats what he shoots and it'd be plumb wrong to waste somethin' as tasty as a teal."

For the first time in several minutes the knot in my stomach relaxed and my throat stopped forming more lumps to swallow. "Thanks officer. I'll try to be more careful next time when a flock that size sails over my decoys."

He picked up my decoy bag and together we started walking along the edge of the pond toward the trail which would return us to the two rut sand road.

"I've got one more question to ask", the warden began, "Ain't ya scared to use yer dog in this swamp?"

I stopped walking and looked blankly at the officer. "Why? What's there to be scared of?"

"Yer a Yankee, ain't ya?"

I nodded, and grinned.

"This here swamp and pond is full ah 'gators. When they're on the prowl for somethin' ta eat, especially before daylight, yer dog'd be easy pickins. I'd say you've been lucky so far."

My grin vanished. "You're kidding me,......aren't you?"

"No, 'gators ain't nothin' ta kid about. Wanna see one?"

Well, dad often said, "Seeing is believing", so I accepted his offer.

The warden put down my bag of decoys and pulled a large folding knife out of his pants pocket. Walking to the edge of the wooded area he cut down a small sapling of some sort and whittled a sharp point on one end. Then he slowly walked along the edge of the water for a few yards, stopped, and motioned for me to come.

"Look down there in the weeds. See that big grove in the bottom ah the pond. She leads right under the sod that's under our feet."

I looked. Back in Wisconsin I had seen entrances to beaver dens that looked just like what I was looking at. "What is it?"

"It's a tunnel leading to a 'gator den. Stand right here and watch. I'll flush the bugger out."

The warden retreated a few feet and began poking his sharp sapling into the soft grass covered soil.

After a half dozen jabs or so, he stopped, looked at me and grinned saying, "Look sharp, he's gonna come out."

With that he gave a mighty thrust with his spear, sinking it into the soil about three feet. The earth beneath my feet trembled slightly and before my startled eyes out of the den zoomed an alligator about ten feet long! I jumped backwards from the waters edge, and uttered, "Holy Shit"! The warden laughed.

After my heart rate returned to normal I had a question to ask. "Say, by any chance do alligators make a sound like a bull frog croaking?"

"Ya, a real BIG bullfrog."

We resumed our journey and within several minutes were back at my car. As we shook hands I asked two more questions.

"Where's your car? Do you need a lift?'

"Nope. My truck's just around the corner up the road a piece. There's another trail up there leading to the far side of the pond. I'll walk. Need the exercise. Good talkin' with ya, young fella. And watch out for them 'gators!"

On the ride home I had ample opportunity to digest all that had happened in one short afternoon. Then it downed on me I had not even asked his name! But whoever he was, I'd bet he was one hell of a good game warden! Most of them are!

And by the way, that was my last hunt in Alligator Alley. I love duck hunting but I love my dogs more!

Carelessness vs Common Sense

More than a few times Dad Anderson and/or my uncles lectured me about "carelessness vs common sense" in regards to hunting and just generally living in the out of doors. Many years ago it were the dads, granddads, and uncles who taught Junior and Sissy the "right way" to hunt, and also be safe while handling firearms. Additional instruction included a liberal dose of "respecting Nature's things and your fellow man". But somehow, as time drifted along, our society just seemed to lack the time and the desire to continue the tradition in an adequate manner. It seems to me making money and having a "good time" often take precedent over spending quality time guiding our youth down the right paths.

Today, In an attempt to eliminate, or at least reduce, carelessness among sportspersons who hunt or use firearms, most states now require youngsters to take and successfully pass a course commonly labeled "Hunter Safety". And having been a licensed hunting and firearms safety instructor since 1968, I know from first hand experience the program works!

"Common Sense" is a bird of another feather. To my knowledge it can't be taught. Or at least nobody has yet figured out how to teach it. Either you got it or you ain't! Dad and Mom Anderson had lots of common sense, and I like to think a bit of those genes were passed on to their son. On the subject of common sense, dad had a short sermon.

"Do what seems to be the right thing to do and generally you won't get into trouble".

Generally!

****

Besides hunting the vast marshlands of the St. John's River, plus numerous water filled sink holes and small inland lakes throughout Central Florida, I discovered another virtually untapped wetlands along Florida's east coast. The Indian and Banana Rivers, which make up portions of the Intercostals Waterway, teamed with waterfowl during the late fall and winter months.

The stretch between Titusville and Cocoa Beach was especially interesting, as the Cape Canaveral Space Center was located nearby and often a visiting duck hunter would be entertained by a pre-dawn missile launch. When a launch took place, the first warning was a slight vibration of the earth beneath your feet, quickly followed by an intense glow of light and flames. Then a deafening roar would full the air and a huge projectile would slowly rise above the horizon, then gain speed as it sped downrange or headed towards outer space.

Missile launches were a big help to waterfowl hunters, as within a few seconds of the launch every known specie of bird would be airborne. Frightened fowl would continue to fly haphazard up and down the river system for a good half-hour or more after each launch, attempting to locate a safe haven.

Early one morning during Christmas Break, my fifteen-year-old neighbor, Bruce, plus Duke and I headed for the coast. The pre-dawn drive took almost an hour, but highway 46 was as usual, nearly devoid of traffic. We launched my Old Town canoe at the public boat ramp near Titusville, attached my little three horse power Johnson motor, and loaded with equipment slowly chugged to a small outcropping of ancient coral in the center of the Indian River.

Earlier in the season I had thrown together a small blind on the island, which Bruce made some minor repairs on as I positioned a modest raft of bluebill decoys. Duke splashed around the island sniffing every square inch with his usual impatient demeanor.

The morning hunt went well. And although no missiles were launched, numerous divers launched themselves without the aid of any external stimulants.

During one exchange of gunfire Bruce crippled a bluebill that turned out to be a real diver. Duke gave chase, but I quickly called him back as the duck was widening the distance between the pursuer and the pursued. I dragged our canoe from hiding, quickly attached the motor, and prepared to retrieve the crippled duck.

Bruce, who had downed the bird had other ideas. "Hey Andy, let me go get 'um."

I hesitated for a moment, then approved Bruce's request. Carelessness had reared it's ugly head.

As Bruce pushed the craft towards deeper water and eased himself in, I added, "Put on your life vest and BE CAREFUL!"

Bruce started the outboard motor and soon was within range of the diving bluebill. Now comes the part about "common sense".

The law clearly states that when pursuing a crippled duck or goose with a boat or canoe, one may not shoot while a motorized craft is under power. The law further states the motor must be shut off and raised up so the shaft and propeller are above the water. I totally understand the reason for shutting off the motor, but why the shaft and prop need to be surrounded by air is a puzzler. But, the law is the law.

Bruce shut off the motor before he shot, but did not raise it. He waited for the duck to surface, and then cleanly ended the chase. Smiling, he returned to the island, we hid the canoe and continued the hunt.

By nine a.m. we were slowly motoring back to the launch area with our limit of ducks and feeling mighty cocky about our success. But that feeling was about to change!

Besides my station wagon, one other vehicle was parked in the launch parking lot. It was a Jeep with "Federal Wildlife Officer" emblazoned on it's side. Also, a monstrous spotting scope rested atop a tripod on the Jeep's hood. Two uniformed officers were positioned on either side of the vehicle.

Having been checked by game wardens on a number of other outing, both while fishing and hunting, I knew the officers were simply doing their job. And having nothing to hide, or so I thought, I smiled and hailed the duo a "Good Morning".

The two wardens slowly walked to the water's edge and as we crawled out of the canoe, then sternly asked to see our licenses. I quickly produced mine, and told the officers my partner was under the age of sixteen and didn't need a Federal Duck Stamp. Our licenses were checked and returned without comment. Next they examined our ducks.

After finding all our birds were legal and within the legal daily limit, the senior officer got to the point. "You two did some nice shooting this morning. And that big Lab or yours is some retriever! We don't see many Labs around these parts."

I grinned and replied, "Thanks. Yes, if you're going to be a duck hunter you should have a good retriever. Saves a lot of cripples. Old Duke here is top drawer."

"Speaking of retrieving,....the boy there made a little mistake when he motored out to get that crippled bluebill."

My mind quickly replayed the event, and then it hit me! Bruce had not pulled the motor's shaft and prop free of the water before he shot the cripple. I silently thought, "Picky, picky, picky. Are we going to get a fine for such a minor violation?" Then I went on the offensive.

"Yes, I realize he goofed officer. The boy did make a little mistake. I should have gone after the duck myself, (although I probably wouldn't have pulled the motor up either) but the boy shot it and wanted to be the one to retrieve it. He's young and still learning the ropes."

"Well, what he did was certainly minor, and I'm not going to make a Federal Case out of it. Everything else we watched you do was legal and ethical, so I'll overlook that small infraction."

Bruce was busy trying not to look scared by shuffling his feet around in the sand, so I thanked the officer for using common sense and breathed an internal sigh of relief. But there was more to come!

"Could you remove your firearms from their cases so we might inspect them?"

"Certainly officer." I knew what was coming next, and was certain both of our shotguns were legal.

Bruce and I unzipped our cases and carefully handed the weapons to the officers. Bruce was using an ancient single shot twelve gauge. The younger officer opened the breech and noted the gun was unloaded. He handed it back to Bruce and muttered something about not seeing many shotguns of that type or vintage. Bruce just grinned.

Next, my Wingmaster 870 underwent a total check. First the chamber was opened and inspected. It was unloaded, as the law, both written and unwritten, requires. Next, the officer began to check the magazine to see if I had installed a "plug" to restrict the magazine's capacity to two shells. Federal law limits the capacity of any gun used for hunting waterfowl to be limited to a total of three shells. One in the chamber and two in the magazine.

The first test shell disappeared into the magazine, then the second. The warden then pushed a third shell into the magazine's opening. It stopped when the first shell struck the internal "plug". The officer then pushed a bid harder. To my horror there was a crunching noise and the third shell also slid into the magazine! And in a flash I recalled a bit of carelessness that now came back to haunt me!

Before the waterfowl season had begun I had used my shotgun for hunting quail and doves. When hunting those species a "plug" is not required, as there is no limit on the number of shells one might place in their gun. I had removed the sturdy wooden plug and forgotten to replace it when the waterfowl season opened.

My memory had returned concerning the missing plug on the opening day of waterfowl season once I reached my blind and prepared to load my faithful 870. In desperation I cut a slender branch off a sapling and manufactured what I intended would be a temporary plug. But due to carelessness and procrastination, the temporary plug become permanent. The slender twig had evidently dried out and snapped when the warden applied too much pressure.

Upon hearing the "crunch", and watching the third shell slip into the magazine, the warden cast a suspicious eye towards the gun's owner and asked, "Now what do you call this?" The tone of his voice was not friendly.

For several seconds the only sound my vocal cords could produce was a stuttering "Dah, dah, dah." But finally I managed to meekly attempt to explain why my plug had crunched.

I asked the warden to hand me my shotgun so I might take it apart and show him I indeed did have a plug in the magazine, such as it was prior to the "crunch". He unloaded the weapon and handed it back to me with a look on his face like a wife questioning her husband returning home in the wee hours of the morning with lipstick on his collar.

I unscrewed the magazine cap, carefully removed the split ring and magazine spring, then turned the gun upside down and dumped out the shattered remains of the slender twig that once had served as my plug. The senior warden picked up the pieces and easily crunched them in his hand. Whatever type of wood I had used, after drying out it lost any strength it once had when it was green.

The warden looked at me and his face softened. "Guess your explanation was valid. Ya know, some violators use what we refer to as a break away plug. Yours just plain broke. I strongly suggest you put a REAL plug in your gun before you head out duck hunting again." He finished with a grin.

The officers said their good-byes, got in their Jeep and drove away.

Bruce and I loaded up our gear, secured the canoe on my car tops and headed home. We were quite quiet for several miles. I broke the spell by telling Bruce we had been lucky to run into a veteran warden with good common sense. And I further explained that generally common sense will overcome certain forms of carelessness.

And our morning hunt had produced two excellent examples!

Odd Ball Duck, "One in a Million"

This tale first appeared in a publication I co-authored and edited for during the early 1980's. THE GUIDES' JOURNAL enjoyed a five year run, and supplied the sporting public with some great outdoor stories and tips. But, the publishing business is a tough nut to crack, and although the project was not a total economic failure, the time necessary to finish each ongoing edition sapped even my then youthful energy, and the project was abandoned.

Some hunters seek only trophies, others like to simply eat what they shoot. I personally like to do both, but my main reason for hunting is it allows me to spend quality time with Ma Nature and all her creatures. A "trophy", like beauty, is in the eye of the beholder. To me, any wild animal or bird is unique and therefore a trophy. End of the editorial.

But this tale, about this hunt, is sure to suggest to any duck hunter that on this day, a genuine trophy was bagged.

Peggy, as well as a host of others, have often accused me of having "duck blood" in my veins. I guess anything is possible. These accusations generally begin sometime in early to mid September and have occasionally continued into January. Somehow this seems to coincide with the migratory waterfowl season in North America.

After our move to Florida, where I spent the next seven school terms attempting to teach U.S. History and Civics to eighth and ninth graders, a new hobby leaped into my life. I began dabbling in taxidermy.

Duck season in the Southland, generally begins late in the year and often runs into January. Therefore, most of the adult birds are in full plumage. And just about every specie of duck found east of the Mississippi River spend part of their winters in the Gulf Coast. My lofty goal was to mount a pair of every species. And I was well on my way when November 29, 1964 rolled around.

****

It was a very typical Sunday in central Florida, one a duck hunter would describe as "A Bluebird Day". A cloudless royal blue sky, beyond any shade of blue one could experience in the northern latitudes, stretched from horizon to horizon. The leaves on my two palm trees next to our carport hung motionless. Cutting the grass clad only in shorts, a t-shirt and thongs left me sweating profusely.

Peggy had been called to work at the super market where she was employed, and grandma had picked up up our two youngsters to take them,......who knows where.

Duke paced back and forth in his spacious fenced in private dog yard as I took a shower, and pondered the boredom. Across the street Bruce Kilmer was just finishing cutting his parent's lawn. We waved at each other and suddenly the urge struck. It was duck season, and an entire lazy afternoon lay before me.

"Hey Bruce! Wanna go shoot some ducks?" What a silly question!

"Yea! Let me ask mom if it's o.k.!"

Bruce was fifteen. He was a nice kid from a home, how shall I put it? Well, he lived in a house that wasn't quite a home. If you get the drift. Every time I'd come home from a fishing or hunting adventure Bruce would come racing across the street to see the bounty and hear the story.

A year earlier I had gained permission from his folks to introduce Bruce to the wonderful world of Ma Nature. He became an outstanding student of the out of doors and soon became almost like a son to me. Peggy and I even were allowed to haul him up north to Wisconsin for a summer, where he did some odd jobs around mom's resort and got in a ton of fishing between chores.

Among his dad's meager possessions was an ancient single shot twelve gauge shotgun that had been owned by Bruce's granddad. Although when I first inspected it I thought perhaps it had belonged to Methuselah. But the action was tight and the barrel was not too awfully pitted, and it was bored "full". It would do to kill a duck or two.

Bruce was given the green light to spend the afternoon with his duck hunting neighbor. We quickly loaded my Grumman Sport Canoe on my station wagon, threw in a couple bags of decoys and added one Black Lab who was going bonkers with glee.

Our destination was Lake Monroe, a monster of a lake which is part of the St. Johns River chain of lakes. While hunting "Brahmaville Marsh" several days earlier we had noticed large numbers of ducks dropping into another marshy area a mile or so south of us along the east shore of Lake Monroe. This was an area into which I had never ventured, and today, being a lousy duck day, would be an excellent time to do some exploring.

We reached the launch area on the north shore of Lake Monroe about two thirty and burned up another half hour motoring to the east shore. I turned off my little three h.p. Johnson, raised the shaft and prop out of the water and seated Bruce in the bow. Then we slowly began paddling up one of the many narrow drainage "runs" that criss crossed the low, marshy area.

We jumped a pair of blue winged teal, but opted not to shoot in hopes of locating bigger ducks. Forty-five minutes evaporated. Our only companions were dozens and dozens of coots that scooted across the narrow, twisting canal to seek shelter in the swish grass.

At a long straight stretch, a dozen or so black ducks mixed with mottled mallards jumped about sixty yards out of range. The waterway on which we had been traveling ended where the flock had been resting.

The time was now four p.m. But an hour and a half remained of legal shooting time. Our present hunting method was beginning to look hopeless, so Bruce and I voted to give up jump shooting, return to the edge of the big lake, put out our decoys, make a makeshift blind,..... and hope for the best.

Returning to the shoreline of Lake Monroe we found a great spot to blind up. Several dense clumps of swish grass offered up a perfect duck blind, and a bushy water cypress tree provided a place to hide my boat from the sharp-eyed waterfowl we hoped would venture in our direction.

Bruce put out a dozen or so mallard and pintail decoys while I hid the boat and prepared two clumps of swish grass for human occupation. Several years earlier I had discovered it was best to thoroughly check out thick vegetation BEFORE climbing into it. Water moccasins make poor roommates.

It had to be over eighty degrees! Sweat rolled off our brows. We soaked our hats in the luke warm lake water and let it dribble over our face and down our backs. Flies buzzed. Duke puffed. Crows cawed. No Ducks!

Four thirty passed. A few crows and blackbirds flitted about the marsh.

Five o'clock came. More of the same. Several small V's of large ducks, no doubt fitted with oxygen breathing equipment, passed high overhead on their way to the watery marshes near "Brahmaville Marsh". Bruce and I congratulated each other on our choice of duck hunting locations.

Five ten: One lone ringbill swung wide of our decoys, about ten yards out of range. I pleaded with my caller in my best bluebill voice, but she passed us up for a raft of coots about two hundred yards further down the lake.

Five twenty: Only ten minutes of shooting time remained, and still neither Bruce nor I had busted a cap. All hope was fading away, along with the sun, which was beginning to sink beneath the western horizon.

I was squinting into these last, long rays of sunshine, as I had done many times before, trying somehow to stop its decent. And then I saw him! Gliding towards our decoys on semi-cupped winds a large, long necked duck was rapidly closing the distance between himself and we who had waited so long.

The bird was still about one hundred and fifty yards beyond our decoys, but closing fast. I gave Bruce a hushed "Get down, here comes one!", and we disappeared into our swish grass blinds. Bruce was about fifteen yards to my right and his view was masked by a clump of water cane, making it impossible to see the duck from that angle.

Our last hope of avoiding a skunking seemed to hesitate, and hover in mid-air, as if to land well short of our decoys. I then broke one of my personal rules about calling to incoming ducks. My feeling is, "If they are coming in, shut up and let them come. If they turn and head away, start calling again." It works for me!

From my duck call came a short chuckling mallard feeding call. The lone bird, which appeared to be a pintail or a mallard, changed its mind and continued its inbound flight path on slowly beating wings.

At a range I estimated to be about sixty yards, I received my first look at what I thought to be color. In the fading sunlight it looked like we were dealing with a greenhead. Being a prize in any hunters bag, greenheads were ever more highly prized in Florida. Black ducks and mottled mallards were quite common, but greenheads were few and far between.

The bird was now about forty yards out and swinging to my right into a slight northwest breeze with his landing gears down. The moment of truth was at hand, and seeing Bruce was shut out of the show behind the clump of water cane, the results all hinged on my shot.

I pointed the muzzle of my Wingmaster a couple of feet in front of his bill and loosed one and a quarter ounces of number six lead shot. The bird pitched forward with a broken wing and landed among our decoys with his feet going full speed even before he hit the water!

At the crack of the gun Duke went charging towards our quarry like a runaway freight train. It was a poor match and the duck lost a short race towards the lake's center. Duke, with his head held high, dropped him at my feet with not a feather ruffled.

My first close up look at the bird tricked my eyes into thinking it was a greenhead, as its head feathers did reflect a sheen of emerald green. But as I picked the bird up by its bill I exclaimed, "Wow, it's a drake pintail!" The bill was truly that of a mature drake pintail.

Bruce arrived and was the first to realize what I had in my hand. He had studied my waterfowl identification book very well. With a wide grin spreading across his face, Bruce nearly cracked my back with a slap of congratulations. "Look, you shot a mallard/pintail hybrid!"

Bruce was absolutely correct! My bird had a green head, a pintail bill, wings that were a combination of both, and a long pointed tail that curled! What a beautiful specimen he was!

Since that time, a lot of duck hunting water has passed under my skiff. I've talked to dozens and dozens of veteran duck hunters. I have yet to find one who, at least knowingly, had bagged a mallard/pintail hybrid.

Naturally, I mounted the beauty and it rested in a place of honor among the many other pairs that graced the walls of my den. But unfortunately, during shipment via U-Haul back to Wisconsin, when Peggy and I left the soon to become crowded Orlando area, my hybrid was ruined beyond repair.

But I still have several clear colored photos and 35mm slides to keep the memory vivid. Including one starring the duck, and the retriever who finished the job!

And I'll Have Milk

My friend Eddie started life at a big disadvantage. That is if being able to easily enjoy numerous outdoor activities is the yardstick we are using for measurement. But fortunately for my buddy, eventually he was able to move to another locale that allowed him to "make up for lost time".

The Prolog to this collection of tales introduced you to Eddie. Not that I'm looking for any gold stars for doing so, but I helped introduce him to the wonderful world of duck hunting, and guided him to his first buck.

Over the nearly sixty years we have known each other we've chased just about everything that has fins, fur or feathers. But he, like me, puts duck hunting at the top of his list of favorite outdoor adventures.

For a number of years before Eddie moved from Chicago to LaCrosse, Wisconsin, he made an annual pilgrimage to Northern

Wisconsin to hunt waterfowl with his friend. Generally his trip occurred in early to mid November when the divers were southbound.

On this particular hunt we shared an experience that Eddie somehow still finds highly amusing, even though it took place about thirty duck seasons ago. And when Eddie and I are together he somehow always finds someone to tell the tale to, just to watch me squirm.

Hell, what are friends for anyway?

****

We were sure we'd have a good day when our canoe hit the thin layer of ice once we left the channel that flows between Upper and Lower Allequash Lake. But then, we weren't surprised, as the mercury in the thermometer at my house, which was nailed to an old red pine, was nestled well into the low teens.

As we paddled into a brisk northwest breeze it sent small jets of spray into our overloaded craft, which froze immediately upon anything it came in contact with. What a wonderful duck hunting morning it was going to be!

Twenty minutes of bucking a quartering wind created a bit of sweat on our bodies, which at the time felt pretty nice. We'd pay for that later. Our blind was on a tiny rocky outcropping, which somehow supported a fairly dense grove of speckled alders and marsh grass. My blind was badly in need of repair. While I waded out on the gravel bar which stretched southward from our island, and positioned our three dozen bluebill decoys, Eddie made repairs to what just two weeks earlier had been a really nice blind.

Finishing with the decoy duty, I dragged my canoe into the alders, tipped it over, and scattered a few gobs of grass and dried weeds over its bottom to break up the outline. Then we settled in to wait for legal shooting time.

Behind our small outcropping of granite boulders and gravel was a fifteen-acre bay filled with wild rice. Hopefully, some northern migrants would decide to stop here for breakfast, spot our fakes, and fly by for a look, or set down for a visit. Duke sat out in front of our blind and panted. Eddie and I poured some hot coffee into our ice-cold thermos cups and gulped it down while there was still some warmth in the liquid. We still had nearly a half-hour to wait.

The wind continued to pick up as daylight slowly fought with the darkness of night. As usual, the first early blush of pink along the eastern horizon gradually turned to orange, then yellow, as Old Sol began winning a battle that had been going on for probably several million years.

Our wait was not without encouragement, as we heard a whistle of wings in the gloom above us, causing our pulse rates to increase and goose bumps to pop up on various parts of our anatomy. We drank a second cup of coffee and devoured several chocolate chip cookies. And finally it was time!

As often happens, our expectations were considerably more lofty than eventual reality. Several small flocks of bluebills and a pair of goldeneyes gave our blocks a look from many yards beyond the range of our scatterguns. We consumed the last of our luke warm coffee, polished off the cookies, and began to shiver as the icy jabs of November poked its fingers through our parkas.

Eddie and I began discussing the possibility we might have picked the wrong lake or the wrong blind or the wrong day for a duck hunt. One of us, perhaps both, suggested a warm cafe and a heaping plate of eggs, sausage, toast and hash browns, with a side order of hot coffee might be more productive than staying huddled on a rocky outcropping of granite and freezing our extremities off. But the sound of incoming jets behind us quickly changed our minds!

Over the tamaracks that marked the shoreline of the bay behind us a half dozen 'bills appeared. With wings semi-cupped and dropping rapidly it was apparent they intended to inspect the rice filled bay below them. Seeing our decoys, they began a wide swing to the south, then turned into the wind and drew a bead on our little island.

The northern immigrants closed rapidly and I heard Eddie's safety snap off a split second before mine uttered a faint "click". Just as the birds were ready to set down at the edge of our decoys I whispered, "Let's take 'um!"

Brimstone and fire spewed from the muzzles of our cold gun barrels. In less time that it takes to say "One, two, three", six empty casings lay scattered around our blind and one lone bluebill was rapidly winging its way downwind. The other five were upside down, feet extended, and bobbing in the waves!

As Duke was finishing up the job, Eddie and I shook hands, and slapped each other on the back. Next, each of us attempted to convince the other that "I went three for three". Then we both looked at each other and laughed. Neither of us actually knew who shot which duck, and actually, it didn't really matter.

The unexpected activity prompted us to stay in our rag tag blind for another half-hour. By then the reoccurring image of a gut filling breakfast overcame our desire to gamble that more ducks would appear prior to our freezing to death.

An hour later we were seated in a comfortable booth at the Outdoorsman Cafe in Boulder Junction, Wisconsin slurping hot coffee and wolfing down that plate of breakfast goodies we had envisioned earlier.

Upon finishing our monstrous meal, our waitress brought the bill and asked if there was anything else we would like. Eddie remembered our empty thermos bottles in my truck. Returning with the empties, we handed them to the waitress.

"Make mine black coffee", said Eddie, who drank it that way, pointing to his thermos.

"I'll have milk in mine", I added, as I prefer a tad of liquid "cow" in my java.

We paid the bill, left a generous tip and climbed back into my truck.

"Well", began Eddie, "What hot spot are we going to try this afternoon. We still have three more ducks to shoot. Or are you going to take me back to Alcatraz Island?"

"Let's try Little Star Lake", I replied, with a know it all look on my face. "Remember the goldeneyes and butterballs we got there last year?"

"Oh yea, I like that spot. You're the guide."

We launched the canoe again and once more worked up a bit of a sweat paddling the half-mile to Birch Point. On the way Eddie and I discussed a new strategic plan. I'd drop Eddie off at the blind at Birch Point, help him put out half of our decoys, and then I'd paddle to the boggy west shore and set up shop there. That way we might just help out each other by keeping any birds that dropped in for a look moving around the lake. Stupid northern divers often will not leave a lake when shot at, but wing their way to the next decoy spread looking for company.

By one thirty we were both set and ready. But as it turned out, the ducks weren't ready to visit Little Star Lake.

About two thirty my body was replaying the script from the morning hunt at Allequash. My feet were cold, my fingers were numb, and my upper torso was shivering. It was definitely time for some fresh, hot coffee!

I opened my thermos, unscrewed the cup, extracted the cork, and poured myself a nice ice-cold cup of MILK!

My first thought was our waitress had pulled a dirty trick on us. But then I recalled my instructions to her!

"I'll have milk in mine." And that's what she gave me. While I was laughing at my self-inflicted folly, Duke turned a curious eye in my direction and possibly thought his boss had gone bonkers.

After another fruitless hour of scanning the empty sky, I picked up my decoys and paddled back to Birch Point. After I helped Eddie pick up his decoys, we paddled back to the car and loaded our gear. As we prepared to exit the launch area I asked Eddie if he had any coffee left. No, he didn't.

Then as I started the engine for our return trip to my house, I asked, "How would you like some ice-cold milk?" Upon completing my tale of woe, Eddie laughed all the way home. And he's still laughing!

Always Count Your Decoys

Our two oldest kids, Chris and Cherie, were baptized into the duck hunting fraternity with the waters of the St. Johns River in Florida. Shortly after they shed their diapers I allowed them to tag along as extra baggage in my canoe or sport boat on afternoon duck hunting trips. Naturally, even as very small toddlers, their childhood curiosity was bound to be aroused when dad dragged home a bag full of feathered objects, which were then plucked, cleaned and eventually wound up on their dinner plates.

Upon actually seeing the process from start to finish both siblings began counting the years, months, weeks and eventually days, until they could tote a shotgun into the marsh with dad and begin the initial stage of the project.

Son Chris turned twelve in '71 and shared the family duck blind on Lost Creek with me on opening day. By opening day in '72 Cherie had turned twelve and created a threesome in our blind.

The fever had been passed to a new generation.

****

I couldn't wait to tell our two oldest kids what I had found on my way home from school.

It was late October and every sign was pointing towards an early winter. Actually our normally short summer in the north woods had been even shorter, and unusually cold and rainy. The trend continued into September and October.

Our local population of blacks, mallards, woodies and teal had long since headed south, and for nearly two weeks the marshes and potholes were nearly devoid of ducks. The previous evening's TV weather map indicated a major cold front was plowing its way across Manitoba and Ontario. My heart raced at the prospect the front might just push a few northern ducks our way and make the coming weekend worth spending some time in a duck blind.

The school where I was teaching was twenty-seven miles north and west of where I lived. There were several different routes I could use when traveling to and from my classroom. The Friday afternoon journey home was planned to pass by several lakes where northern migrants often made reservations to spend a few days on their route south. I struck pay dirt at my second stop.

Chris and Cherie were already home when I arrived, glued to the boob tube watching Popeye pound the crap out of Bluto. "Hey kids, guess what your old man found on his way home today."

Without even looking at me I received a response of; "A dead partridge on the road?"

"Very funny. No dead partridge on the road, but about hundred or more butterballs on Little Star."

Two heads snapped around as Popeye tossed a battered Bluto out a second story window. "Are we going after them tomorrow morning?"

"No, we're going to stay home and watch cartoons."

"Very funny dad, Ha, ha, ha."

Plans for the anticipated conquest were discussed at the dinner table, despite the bored looks that radiated from Peggy and our two younger girls. And being girls, they couldn't resist butting into the conversation.

From the mother of our brood; "Could we talk about something else other than hunting while we're having dinner?"

From eight year old Anna; "Who would be so stupid as to get up at four a.m. and then go sit on the edge of some stupid lake and freeze your fanny off?"

From six year old Wendy; "Why would you want to shoot a duck? They seem like nice birds."

From Chris and Cherie; "Shut up and mind your own business, you little twerps!"

Plans were eventually finalized, and our equipment was stashed by the door in the back porch ready to be loaded for transport to the Promised Land early the next morning.

Now I must digress for a moment to remind the reader about teen-aged, (or actually any aged) kids. As parents we have no control over which kid gets which gene. Passing genes from generation to generation could best be described as a crapshoot.

The gene that programs my daily activity is one that commands me to follow the old adage; "Early to bed, early to rise, makes a man, healthy, wealthy, and wise." And I always figured that one out of three is still batting .333.

The gene that programs my wife's daily activity is one that commands: "Sleep late and burn night-lights, your husband's asleep it prevents daily fights." I realize that is NOT an old adage, but I figure if enough people repeat it for enough years, it might have a chance to become one.

I was up at four, letting dogs outside to perform their morning ritual, marking the boundary of their territory. Next came feeding the cat and making coffee and hot chocolate. Four thirty knocks on two additional bedroom doors resulted in securing one wide-awake anxious hunter, which was my daughter. From bedroom two, came a low moaning sound informing me "I'm tired and think I'll pass on this trip. Those butterballs probably won't be there anyway. They probably all flew south."

My son had obviously been passed the recessive gene.

Additional verbal incentives on my part had no visible effect on my son's desire to take part in a chilly late October duck hunt. So the planned threesome became a twosome.

This also happened to be the fall my black Lab was expecting to be a mother. The vet had suggested rather strongly that I not hunt Teal for teal, or any other type of duck. So besides being father and guide, I also would assume the role of retriever. Should there be anything to retrieve.

Cherie and I paddled our canoe across the choppy surface of Little Star Lake under a starless and moonless sky. The birch trees at White Birch Point moaned under the stress of a biting northwest wind. What a perfect morning for divers!

I carefully placed nineteen plastic bluebill decoys fairly close to shore, hoping to entice any ducks that swung our way into venturing close enough for Cherie's little twenty gauge double to make clean kills. My second reason for keeping the decoys close to our blind was to keep me from exceeding the limit of my waders when making a retrieve.

The nearly half-hour wait till legal shooting time passed with the speed of a snail in January. I could tell my daughter was already feeling the chilly pangs of autumn, but she offered no complaints. She sipped her hot chocolate while I gulped down two cups of hot coffee.

Shooting time arrived before there was enough daylight to shoot sensibly. Low, scudding gray clouds skidded across the sky, doing an excellent job of delaying good visibility.

Our first arrivals were a small band of hooded mergansers that appeared out of nowhere and plopped unceremoniously into our plastic fakes. After making a few dives looking for breakfast, they quickly departed for parts unknown. I began to wonder if my son's excuse for not joining in on the hunt might be true. Maybe the butterballs had already checked out of the neighborhood.

Fifteen more minutes ticked by. My earlier certainty of having a successful outing began to wane. But then Cherie tugged at the sleeve of my hunting coat and excitedly whispered, "Here they come dad!"

Off to our right, hugging the surface of the water, a dozen or so small black and white ducks were rapidly bearing down on our decoy spread. "Let 'um land.", I whispered back.

Buffleheads are not known as the Albert Einstein of the duck world. Few varieties decoy as readily as the specie we refer to as "butterballs". (And if you've even dined on buffleheads, you'll know why they're nicknamed butterballs.) And as I expected, the entire flock skidded to a halt at the outer edge of our decoys.

My daughter was still well mired in the beginner's stage when it came to hitting ducks on the wing. So I had told her she could "ground swat" one on the water if we could get some birds to decoy. Then her second shot would have to be taken at a departing target. For young beginners, some degree of success is a necessity in order to build confidence and interest in any sport, not only hunting! And ducks do taste the same whether shot while sitting or flying.

Once the flock landed I whispered one more suggestion. "Take that closest drake, and then pick another bird when they take off."

It seemed like an eternity as I waited for my daughter to line up her target and shoot. But shoot she did, and the shot pattern perfectly centered the unsuspecting migrant. I had pre-picked a second drake, and tumbled him cleanly on take off, then took a hen that was still in range. Cherie had only fired once.

"Did I get him?", she asked, with doubt in her voice.

"Did you get him?", then pointing I added, "Do you think that duck over there is practicing the backstroke?"

A smile a mile wide lit up Cherie's face and with a simple exclamation of "YES!" she concluded her first conquest of the morning.

I unloaded my Wingmaster and carefully leaned it securely in the corner of our blind before I began my added responsibility of being our retriever. I was nearly to the upper limits of my waders by the time I reached her prize. It was then I received an unexpected command from my daughter.

"DAD, don't move! Here come some more ducks!"

I hunched over, trying to make my upper torso as small as possible, and took a peek towards the lakes center. Another band of butterballs was swooping towards us at full throttle. Without hesitation the group plopped into our decoys. I was suddenly surrounded by ducks! Two were almost close enough to pet!

Behind me in the blind I heard snickering. My mind raced, trying to think what I should do next. I decided to begin a dialog with my daughter.

"Cherie, how many are there?"

A few seconds ticked away as the count took place. "I see fourteen."

"Can you shoot one without shooting me also?"

More snickering. "Sure! There's three of them twenty feet to your left."

The ducks nearest me looked at me but seemed totally at ease. Perhaps I was the first human they have ever been in contact with.

"O.K., go ahead and shoot."

At the sound of the shot I quickly looked to my left. One duck was prone on the water and the remainder of the flock sat motionless wondering what in the world made such a loud noise.

Now there were two people snickering.

"Should I shoot another one dad?"

"No, wait. Let me see if I can scare them enough to make them fly. See if you can bang one in the air."

With that, I straightened up, let out a blood-curdling scream, and slapped the water with the dead duck I was holding. The butterballs had seen enough.

Cherie's second shot was right on target, adding one more duck for me to retrieve, along with the other three.

Our hunt lasted but a half-hour longer. My gleeful daughter shot three additional butterballs to round out our legal limit of eight birds. Which was a good thing as she was almost out of ammunition!

While Cherie sipped the last cup of her lukewarm chocolate, I began the task of picking up our decoys. After winding up the strings and securing the lead weights on each bird, Cherie held the gunnysack open and I dropped in the plastic fakes, counting as I dropped.

Although I had set out nineteen decoys, there were but sixteen to put back in the sack. As it turned out, my daughter wasn't much better at hitting ducks on the water than hitting them on the fly. Some of her errant shots had sent three of my decoys to Davy Jones Locker!

Upon reaching the landing my first order of business was to start the truck and turn up the heater. Cherie's cheeks were rosy reds, but still I had heard no complaints.

By the time I loaded all our gear and secured the canoe to the car tops, the cab of the truck was toasty warm. As the first five or six miles of our homeward bound trip disappeared behind us I replayed the morning hunt over and over in my mind. The only thing missing that I wish had happened would have been having Chris along with us. He had missed out on a very memorable morning!

Finally I broke the silence. "Well Cherie, do you think your brother is still in the sack?"

My question was received with stony silence. I turned my head to look at my daughter. Her head was resting on the window of the passenger door. Her eyes were closed in deep sleep. But she face contained just a hint of a contented grin.

And that also was one hell of a wonderful memory!

Dutch Chocolate and The Bluebills

Hank and I became friends soon after he and his family moved to Northern Wisconsin from upper New York State shortly after World War II. It has been a continuing friendship. Both being outdoor fanatics, it was pre-destined that over the many years of our relationship we would share numerous experiences in quest of creatures sporting fur, fin or feather.

We shared many similar traits, and disagreed on but a few. Dogs being one of the few.

When we first met, Hank hunted with an aging Chesapeake, a breed of waterfowl retrievers having few rivals. Pluto was a great retriever, but with the usual small streak of bullheadedness found in many of his kind.

After Pluto passed on to the Big Doghouse in the Sky, Hank hunted without a retriever for many seasons, but finally succumbed to an inner desire to once again acquire a canine companion.

The selection process was long. I interjected my two cents worth, and of course being prejudiced towards Labs, made that suggestion. My input was rebuffed with a simple explanation. "Everybody has a Lab. I want something different."

And he bought an American Water Spaniel.

****

His name certainly fit! Dutch Chocolate matched his color perfectly. And as with all puppies, he was a cute charmer. But puppies, like kids, eventually grow up and develop their own special personality. And generally, that's a good thing. But not always.

Hank worked hard training his new companion during Dutch's formative months. The pup was catching on to commands and doing well during retrieving drills. In fact, Dutch began practicing retrieving objects between the instructional periods set by his master. Hank would often return home from work or play to find retrieved treasures scattered throughout his yard. Included on the list of Dutch's retrieves were objects which belonged to the neighbors, such as bed sheets, pillow cases and assorted articles of clothing plucked from clothes lines. One day a small tent materialized in Hank's back yard. Another time there was a backpack full of animal traps. The neighbors found little humor in Dutch's skill as a retriever. But Hank pressed on with the lessons.

Although the following training event did not take place while Hank was working with Dutch, I choose to include the episode in this tale as a warning to other dog trainers. It's highly probable you'd want to skip this training procedure.

Hank's family purchased Princess, who was a type of sled dog. One evening as Hank and Princess had ended a short training session, the two of them decided on racing a few laps around their home. Twilight had set in as the circular race began. Hank was an exceptional athlete and very fleet afoot. Master secured a fair lead on his student and turned his head to shoot a glance behind him to see just how much a lead he had on his pup. This maneuver took place just as Hank was rounding a corner of his house. Disaster lay just ahead.

Hank actually knew the electrical pole was there, but during the heat of the race, knowing so at the time was non-essential trivia. The next day, as Hank explained how he had acquired a black eye and the lump on his forehead, it was easy to see how such an accident could have taken place. "I turned my head to see where Princess was for a split second, and when I looked forward again,.....there was the pole about six inches from my face."

I recall laughing my head off for several minutes, and made a mental note to cancel any personal plans involving a race with my dog over a course which included electrical poles.

With the advent of duck season Hank and Dutch were primed and ready for action. The two of us generally hunted together on opening weekend, but knowing it is better to keep first time pups and veteran dogs apart in order to allow the pup to work without distractions, we split up.

At the time, Hank and I were teaching at the same institution and rode to work together. On Monday morning, as I navigated the twenty plus mile route to our place of work, we swapped tales of our respective weekend hunts. And I was eager to find out how Dutch performed. In fact, I asked that very question.

"Hey, he did real well. I'm very pleased." There was a pause. I looked at Hank, who was seated in the passenger's seat, and he had a slightly puzzled look on his face. Then he continued. "He's got one little quirk that needs to be straightened out." Another pause.

"What kind of a quirk?"

"He'll only retrieve mallards or black ducks."

My first inclination was this was the beginning of a great duck-hunting joke. "Yea, what's the punch line Hank?"

"No,....I'm serious. My dog will only retrieve mallards and blacks. I shot some ringbills and teal, but all he would do was swim right out to them, give the birds a few sniffs, and return to the blind without retrieving them!"

"You're kidding!"

"No, damn it, I'm not kidding."

"Well, he's still pretty young, he'll probably outgrow it." But still, I was skeptical that any retriever would be so selective as to what type of bird he retrieved. When I lived in Florida, Duke even retrieved turkey buzzards!

My skepticism evaporated later that fall when Hank and I spent some time together in our blind on Rice Lake. Dutch simply did not show any interest in retrieving any species except mallards or black ducks. And these two species he retrieved with relish! This was a mystery of the type I had never heard of before,.......or since.

Another duck season slipped by, and Dutch's little quirk remained unchanged. Hank seemed to be slowly accepting the fact he had a "two duck dog". But his attitude changed one raw November morning in 1976.

My retriever was recovering from a badly cut foot and had been put on the fifteen day disabled list. The timing was terrible, as the northern migrants were streaming south and rafting up on many of their traditional resting and feeding lakes. Hank and I discovered such a location, which contained a substantial number of bluebills during our custom of investigating suspected duck hideouts on our way home from work.

Well before dawn the following morning we parked our vehicle in the parking lot at the launch site on Little John Lake. The launch site is on the north shore, and on that day the wind was roaring out of the northwest. We each shouldered a sack of decoys and made our way down the shoreline to the northwest corner of the lake. Here the lake bottom was fairly firm and decoys could be set in place with the aid of leak proof waders. The shoreline was infested with alders and cattails, making it simple to simply hunker down in the natural vegetation and be totally concealed.

The first wave of 'bills rocketed into our decoy spread shortly after the opening bell. Six spent cartridges left four of their numbers upside down on the water. Dutch Chocolate sprang into action. He swam to duck number one, gave it a sniff, then swam to duck number two and took another sniff. This routine was repeated with ducks three and four. All the while Hank was shouting encouragement. "Good boy,....bring the duck! Good Dutch,...fetch the bird. Please

Dutch, bring that bird here!" I thought possibly Dutch had a hearing disability.

Convinced none of the floating objects were mallards or black ducks, Dutch turned north and headed for sound terra firma. It was at this moment Hank's attitude changed considerably.

I watched with questioning eyes as Hank began kicking the snow covered ground. His boots dislodged a slender long since dead maple sapling. This he gripped like a baseball bat and charged to the edge of the lake, which in my view and also Dutch's, was a threatening posture.

"BRING THOSE DUCKS IN HERE OR I'LL KNOCK YOUR BRAINS OUT!"

Dutch began paralleling the shore, staying well beyond the range of his master's weapon. Hank paced the speed of his dog, not allowing Dutch to reach shore. Dutch reversed his direction, Hank reversed his direction. I leaned against a handy birch tree and began to laugh hysterically.

The game of cat and mouse continued for several minutes. Hank kept reminding Dutch what fate was in store for him should he come ashore without a bluebill in his jaws. Dutch seemed to be tiring, Hank seemed fresh. I slid down the trunk of the birch to a sitting position and jacked up the volume of my laughter.

Dutch, being no dummy, finally compromised. He gently seized the wing tip of the nearest duck, swam to shore, released his grip on the duck, and made his escape into the forest!

Hank turned and looked at his hunting buddy, who was now clutching his sides and howling with unrelenting laughter. Rarely have I viewed such a comedy routine! Not being sure that I would not receive the same fate as had been promised to Dutch, I gradually downscaled my laughter to simply gasping for oxygen.

The long maple sapling did save the day, as we were able to reach the other three ducks with the device. Then realizing we had no canoe or boat to retrieve additional birds that might fall too far out in the lake, or worse yet, be crippled, we picked up our decoys and returned to Hank's truck.

Dutch was cowering under its protection, but by then all was forgiven and master and dog completed their reconciliation.

Dutch did not outlive his quirk. Hank did not obtain another American Water Spaniel, or any other retriever. To this day, he does that task himself.

I, on the other hand, am well into my sixth Black Labrador Retriever!

Test Your Handloads BEFORE Using

It's funny in a way, that generally a person begins to actually take notice of seemingly insignificant things only after middle or old age sets in. At least that's been my personal observation. It wasn't until I reached that stage of my life before I began to recall that numerous writers, songwriters, and even a politician or two have stated that very concept. One of my favorite lines referring to this phenomenon was penned and sung by the country/western crooner, Tom T. Hall, who wrote and sang a ditty entitled "Faster Horses, Younger Women, Stronger Whiskey".

Now how does that translate into what I'm implying? Simple! Let's use duck hunting as an example, and use ammunition as the specific item to prove what Tom claimed happens to us as we march along the twisting path of life.

When we're young and stupid, the rookie duck hunters generally buy whatever shells are the cheapest. Their goal is to be able to shoot at some ducks, but save a little $$$$ for beer, and gas for the "chick wagon". The next evolutionary step, after we discover our cheap game loads wound more ducks than they kill, is to buy "heavy loads", which if used at sensible ranges, does the job. Later still, we reach the stage in our evolution when the Madison Avenue Advertising Sharks have convinced us "Bigger and Faster" are the only way to go if you want to be a macho male.

The next step is to custom hand load your ammunition!

****

Hank and I hit the "Handloading Plateau" in our lives when we were in our mid-thirties. Which, looking back on that era is right on schedule when most men seem to reach the "Mighty Macho" stage of their lives. (If you're lucky, it's a short era.)

After reading much drivel in the "Big Three" outdoor magazines of the day about handloading, we were convinced we'd kill more game and even save big bucks by loading our own ammo. We had been bitten by the sharks.

It wasn't until we unloaded all the necessary expensive equipment and tallied up the bill that we realized the amount we had expended would have purchased enough factory duck loads to last us ten or fifteen seasons. So we lied to our wives about how much we spent and set up our new Mec 600 Jr. loader in my basement.

Actually, building our own custom shotgun shells was fun. We took turns pulling the handle and puffing up with pride as each finished product came off the assembly line and was placed lovingly in a cardboard box that said "Remington Express" or Peter's High Velocity", or "Winchester Super Speed" on them. Some, (actually most) of the crimps looked a bit amateurish, but surely, we thought, that would not effect the performance of our handloads. Next, we needed to test our product before we hit the marsh on opening day.

The clay pigeon thrower and several crates of clay pigeons drained off a bit more of our limited budgets, but we REALLY did need to see how our homemade bullets worked. For several days prior to the traditional duck season opener, rumors persisted around the area that a group of armed militia members had moved into the neighborhood.

Opening weekend went well. We didn't kill anymore nor less ducks than normal, but hunting just seemed to be a little more fun when using your very own personal brand of shells. Our companions on the marsh were curious about what brand of ammunition we were using.

At days end, as the opening day throng converged at the launch area to swap stories and lie about their shooting skills, that very question cropped up several times,.....followed by mirthful snickers.

"Hey, what kind of shells were you guys using anyway? Almost every shot sounded different. One would go "bang", the next one, "blam", then "pop", or, "pooffff". And after you guys emptied out on a flock there was so much smoke it looked like your blind was on fire. You're not using black powder are you?"

Hank and I assumed these wise guys were simply jealous of our powerful handloads.

Still we pressed on, turning out an ever increasingly better looking product. But could it be possible to build an ever better and MORE POWERFUL duck load? The guy behind the counter in the reloading department at "Bill's House of Guns" had the answer to our question!

The gallon can of Al-can 7 powder and two new charge bars actually didn't place us in danger of bankruptcy, but we agreed to keep this little secret hidden from the wives.

We ran into a slight problem during the first test run with our new reloading formula. The amount of powder filled too much of the casing, causing half of the shot to dribble out on our reloading bench! A short conference was held. Any idiot could see the problem was with our wad column. The thickness of the fiber wads we were using was taking up too much space in the hull!

Another trip to the reloading department solved our problem. Several boxes of those new fangled plastic shot sleeves followed us home. And, just like the expert at the gun shop said, "It solved our problem." But what he didn't tell us was a different problem was lurking in our hand loads!

Now that we had become masters of the handloading art, testing new loads was totally unnecessary. Besides, those new loads kicked like a mule, and who would want to damage ones shoulder prior to hunting season? Without question, these new powerful hand loads would surely kill ducks at ranges only thought possible with air to air missiles.

By opening day we had accumulated nearly a case of our new wonder shells! Boy, would the ducks be in trouble this season! Actually, it wasn't the ducks that were in trouble, it was the macho men on the other end of the gun.

We passed off our poor shooting during the early part of the season with excuses of "too windy", "didn't have my cheek down on the stock", "I'm wearing too many clothes", "guess they were further than we thought", etc. etc. You know the list.

We did hit birds, but way too many were cripples. And both of us were blowing way too many close in "no brainer" shots! And when we had to shoot at the numerous cripples we produced, the shot pattern seemed to be very thin. We made up more excuses.

It was well into mid November before we fully realized SOMETHING was seriously wrong with our new power loads. The event occurred on the way home from our teaching jobs late one snowy afternoon. Stopping to check out "Pothole # 9", we gleefully discovered a dozen or so mallards and black ducks feeding close to shore along the leeward side of the pond. We quickly changed into our hunting garments, uncased our faithful scatterguns and began the stalk.

The sneak was simple. We crawled to within fifteen yards of the unsuspecting migrants using the ample natural vegetation along the banks of the pond to screen our slow, deliberate journey. On a whispered count of "three", Hank and I rose as one. The flock of startled ducks rose as one. And all but two made a clean get away!

Both birds we knocked down were crippled, and several additional shells were expended in finishing the job. My partner and I looked at each other in utter disbelief. How could we miss such easy shots? There was no excuse known to man, which would explain such terrible shooting. And although neither of us were

National Champions of Wing Shooting, we were at least average. A blind hunter could have hit those birds!

After wading out and gathering in our meager harvest I mentioned a reoccurring vision I remembered which took place as we were shooting at our two cripples on the water.

"Say Hank, when you shot your last shot at your cripple, it looked like something hit the water about fifty yards out and then skipped a couple of times. Kinda like Charles Atlas had skipped a rock across the pond. You don't have any slugs mixed up with your duck loads, do you?"

"No, I don't even own any slugs. Now that you mention it, I thought I saw something like that happen a couple of other times lately. Maybe some fish were jumping as we shot."

"Ya, that's probably it. Some fish jumped." But what I had witnessed were certainly not fish jumping. The mystery deepened.

As we were walking along the shore headed back to where we had parked our vehicle, a lone bluebill hove into view and began circling the pond. The duck was high, as indicated by the faint vapor trail it was producing. My buddy, with a joking grin on his face said, "Watch this. I'm gonna pop that bluebill." Hank raised his Model 12 and touched off a shot for what he had been intended to be a joke.

There was a visible puff of feathers from the high-flying bluebill, and it folded up like it had run into a brick wall. Two sets of jaws dropped open as the bird plummeted earthward and splashed down but twenty yards from where we stood in amazed silence!

Upon retrieving the bird, a close examination greatly heightened our suspicions that something was very wrong with our hot handloads! The breast of the bluebill was ripped open as though a rifled slug had struck! In fact, we double checked our pockets to make sure we didn't have some slugs mixed in with our handloads. We didn't!

It was apparent we needed to do some long overdue testing on our power loads!

The next evening I fired a round into a soft sand hillside next to my garage. There was a definite hole in the sand where my charge of number six's had struck. My fingers soon found the object that had created the hole. Again, my jaw dropped open in amazement and initial disbelief!

The plastic shot cup had been partially melted by the heat produced by the powder under it, fusing together about half of the shot inside the shot cup. In reality, we had been shooting slugs at ducks all fall! Only a small percentage of the shot pellets were leaving the gun barrel as individual pellets! No wonder our shooting was causing so many cripples!

Now it was back to the drawing board. By adding a thin felt wad under the plastic cup, and reducing the powder charge a tad, all returned to normal.

A few years later the use of lead shot for hunting waterfowl was banned. And that new rule put an end once and for all to our practice of producing our own personal hand loads. And,....that was a good thing!

"4th of July" Morning

It may come as a surprise to many non-hunters, and probably all "anti" hunters, that actually most hunters go hunting for reasons other than simply killing something.

But, as always there is often an exception. For very young or inexperienced hunters, frequently the killing of game is what drives the sport. A parallel would be giving a teen-ager their first credit card and dropping them off at the Mall Of America for a few hours. I'll be the first to admit that when I began my long journey through the various stages a hunter passes through, shooting something was the upper most reason for the hunt. The eating what you shot was second. Hunting just to kill something is "Stage One". But the early immature attitude soon fades to be replaced by additional and more sophisticated emotions.

Stage Two lasts much longer, provided the hunter becomes addicted to the sport and practices often to hone his or her skills. The urge to hunt only to kill things becomes less and the hunter becomes more selective, such as only harvesting game that is favored at the dinner table. At this stage, the quantity of the harvest often plays a large role in rating the success of a hunt. Stage two also includes an urge to hunt with certain special individuals, such as dad or mom, or a sibling, or gramps, or a close buddy, or maybe uncle somebody.

Stage Three usually begins during the hunter's third or fourth decade of life. Now the hunt is often for very specific game. Possibly a trophy, or a certain something to hang on the wall of a den. Quantity is slowly replaced by quality. More time is spent on the planning, and more time in deep contemplation about what it means to take a life of any living creature, even though the earth's animals spell food and survival for mankind.

Stage Four finds the veteran hunter placing the most value on "The Going", and whom he or she goes with. The amount of time spent in the field, forest or marsh on individual hunts is often less than before. And the pleasure gained from the experience is measured by many intangibles that are impossible to explain to a non-hunter. Only those who have experienced a life a field with companions, gun and dog will know what I'm trying to say. During stage four of a hunter's life, he cares not if he draws a blank during the hunt. The harvest of game become anti-climatic to The Going and The Being There!

There is one other factor that often begins to occur sometime during the Stage Two era, and will continue throughout the remainder of the hunter's career. If it is possible to pull a fantastic, non-dangerous, practical joke on a hunting companion,.....go for it!

****

Great gifts often come in small packages. I received one such valued treasure on a warm June afternoon when a lifelong pal unexpectedly dropped by my house for a visit. I'll call him Bob, although that is not his actual name. Bob was a career military man, and we had seen very little of each other since our graduation from high school. But during our teen aged years we had spent a considerable amount of time together doing what teen-aged boys generally do, and that included a ton of hunting.

Two hours evaporated quite quickly as we relaxed on my sun-drenched deck, draining a few brewskis, and dredging up old memories of happy times past. We re-killed lots of ducks, deer, grouse, rabbits, and once again landed a basket full of brook trout. Between the shooting and the catching, we allowed our memories to retreat back in time to recall wonderful experiences we shared while building and playing in The Mother of All Tree Houses!

Bob had other affairs to attend to later that afternoon, so I walked him to his car to say another "good-bye". But before he departed, Bob handed me one of the most unique and useful gifts I have ever received!

"Hey, I almost forgot!", Bob exclaimed as he snatched a small brown bag off the dashboard of his vehicle. "I get these from our quartermaster at the base. I thought you'd find a good use for them."

I was immediately suspicious, as Bob's face radiated a grin from ear to ear.

Cautiously I opened the bag and peeked inside. Six twelve gauge shotgun shells rested in the depths of the container. I extracted one, and looked it over carefully. The paper casing was dull red, without any visible markings of any kind. The top wad was likewise vacant of information. I then looked at the bottom of the brass base where the primer is located. There were several letters and numbers, which appeared to be some sort of code.

"What the hell are these?", I asked with a puzzled look on my face.

Bob laughed. "Well, they're strictly military stuff. You might say they're a twelve gauge Roman Candle."

"A what?"

"The military uses them to scare unwanted animals and birds off our runways to help avoid plane and critter collisions. The shell fires a ball of explosives at the unwanted visitors, or fired up into the sky to scare off seagulls or other unwanted birds at our landing fields. The navy also used them as flares. When fired at night they look like something you'd see at a 4th of July celebration. Have some fun with them, but if someone inquires where you got 'um, it wasn't me!"

We shook hands, Bob drove off, and as the old saying goes, "Left me holding the bag."

Darkness couldn't come quickly enough. I couldn't wait to try one out. About ten p.m. I stepped out onto my deck, slipped one of the mystery cartridges into the chamber of my trusty twelve gauge, pointed the muzzle towards the night sky, and pulled the trigger.

There was a modest "pooofff" sound and almost no recoil. A bright streak of light rose swiftly into the night sky. And then at an altitude of about a hundred yards there was a brilliant explosion of colored streamers quickly followed by a highly audible, "BOOOOOM"! It was awesome!

As I walked back into the house my mind began planning an excellent use for Bob's gift!

October finally arrived, and with it the long awaited opening of duck season. Hank and I spent the week end opener together at our blind on Rice Lake, and had our usual wonderful time, plus killed a few ducks. I spent part of the weekend closely watching Hank's routine, and plotting how I was going to pull off my planned prank. Early one Saturday morning several weeks later I was presented with a golden opportunity!

The northern ringbills had arrived! Rice Lake was full of them, and the flocks needed some pruning. Hank and I arrived at the landing much earlier than necessary to make sure we'd arrive ahead of the other groups of locals that were sure to show up knowing what we knew. And we wanted the choice location. A ten-minute paddle brought us to Tamarack Point. We quickly set out two dozen bluebill decoys, plus a dozen oversized mallard fakes, just in case some of those orange legged northern mallards or blacks were also in the neighborhood.

Once we were tucked into our blind, I whined a tad about the fact some of the grass we had woven into the alders that formed the substance of the blind had blown away. I gently suggested we harvest some marsh grass and make the repairs before the ducks arrived. Hank ventured out to start the harvest, but I hung back for a few additional seconds.

I quickly opened Hank's small duffle bag and located his box of number six heavy loads. I scooped off the top layer and replaced it with five of Bob's Roman Candles. Then I closed the box and helped harvest some marsh grass.

The repair party finished the minor task in a few minutes and then settled back into the blind once more to guzzle some coffee, dunk some stale donuts, and make small talk while we waited for the eastern sky to blush.

As we consumed our coffee we noted several additional vehicles arrived at the launch area and their occupants paddled off in various directions to await the morning flight. Several flicks of light from our flashlight informed the late arrivals that Tamarack Point was occupied. It was almost a certainty that every hunter on the lake were locals and no doubt we all knew each other. That turned out to be true, and another plus I had factored into my overall prank plot.

A few minutes before shooting time we opened our shell boxes and loaded our weapons. It took all my inner effort to refrain from laughing at what I knew was soon to happen!

The first flock of ringbills arrived slightly before shooting time and circled the lake several times trying to decide which spread of decoys they wished to join. The wind was perfect for the blind on Tamarack Point!

With the sound of air rushing over beating wings the flock made a turn into the wind and zeroed in on our location. I looked at my watch and noted the magic moment had arrived. I whispered a suggestion to my companion and snapped off my safety to let him know I was serious. "Let's take 'um, they're going to fly right over our blind."

We stood in unison and swung our gun barrels up and in front of the low flying, unsuspecting migrants. As one, we each pulled the trigger.

My gun roared, and a chunky ringbill folded cleanly. Hank's gun gave off a soft "pooofff" sound, followed by a streak of light that zoomed upward and through the flock of ducks, causing the group to split into two smaller bunches. And it's highly probable they were scared enough to lighten their load a tad! The streaking light suddenly turned into a blob of bursting colors, accented by "BOOOOM". The colored streamers then began to flutter earthward and one by one were extinguished during their downward glide.

It took every ounce of energy to contain my emotions. But I needed to withhold my gleeful laughter that was bottled up inside me for just a bit longer.

The initial look on my companion's face was one to remember. With eyes the size of silver dollars, Hank stared at his Model 12, then looked at me, and said, "What in the hell was that?"

My laughter began to seep out as I managed to reply, "Boy that was some hand load, What did you load it with?"

"Hand load, Hell, I'm shooting factory ammo!" Hank then pumped out a second cartridge and examined it for several seconds. He turned to me and hissed, "You, (bleeping bleep)! What are these?"

His remarks unleashed all my pent up mirth. I laughed until tears flowed down my cheeks like miniature waterfalls. My laughter triggered Hank's sense of humor and he joined in with hysterical giggling. When I was finally able to croak out the answer to his question, the laughter once again began and continued unabated until our sides ached.

Finally we settled down and returned to the business at hand. By eight a.m. we were picking up the decoys and admiring our limit of ringbills.

Several other hunters were packing their vehicles when we arrived at the landing and they had some questions to ask us about the opening salvo of gunfire from Tamarack Point.

Additional laughter occurred upon hearing our explanation.

That was the only time I used Bob's gift to pull off a practical joke. The remaining four mystery rounds were shot into the air off my deck to ring in the New Year. Hank and his wife were in attendance to view the midnight spectacle, but the show paled by comparison to the October morning mischief in the marsh.

Prairie Potholes

The world contains countless beautiful places in which to hunt ducks, or participate in any other outdoor activities in which you'd care to indulge. For we who live in America, whether it is North or South America, let us be thankful Ma Nature provided Homo sapiens with ample space to "do our outdoor thing", whatever it may be.

I would guess the vast majority of outdoor enthusiasts, like myself, dream of numerous localities we would like to visit during our brief moment in time here on Earth. I would further guess this vast majority, like myself, lack two basic commodities which would allow them to actually visit all the special places we can only dream about. Those commodities are time and money.

But even "middle class Joe" can expand his or her horizons with journeys to new places and new adventures with enough planning and desire. And by planning a "bare bones" trip, it won't cost an arm and a leg or a second mortgage on your home.

****

For me, retirement has been good! Very good in fact. I closed the door on my classroom in June of 1996, after spending thirty-six school terms behind one. And I left with no regrets, and many, many great memories!

My only minor complaint about having to work at any nine to five job, or in my case seven thirty to three thirty, is that it really cuts deeply into having enough time for enough "fun in the fall". However, that is no longer a problem!

My maiden voyage to Manitoba in 1958 was still a vivid memory, even thirty-eight years later when I said my farewell to the educational system. That trip had been a fulfilling of one of my earliest dreams. Retirement allowed me to make a few more of my dreams become reality!

In September of 1997 five of my close companions and myself completed a caribou hunt in Quebec. We saw some of the most spectacular wilderness in North America. However, the weather was much too warm for that time of year and the caribou migration was stalled fifty miles to our northeast. The group did bring home six of the magnificent animals, but four of the six hunters never fired a shot. I being one of the four. But, a great time was had by all. The memories of the flight in and out, the great food and camaraderie, poker games, catching and eating fresh brook trout and lakers, and an unlimited amount of fresh air and elbowroom are memories to cherish forever.

October of 1998 found me hunting high in the San Juan Mountains of Colorado with four of my pals hunting the majestic Rocky Mountain Elk. This, without a doubt, turned out to be "My Personal Hunt of a Lifetime", not counting the seven hours spent on horseback getting to and returning from our tent camp.

We spent eight glorious days in the wilderness, and were treated to just about every "mood of the mountains" the Rockies can toss your way. We arrived in a blizzard with lightning and thunder. We hunted for two days in our t-shirts, and viewed the golden aspens bathed in brilliant sunshine beneath cloudless blue skies.

We endured nearly thirty-six hours of continuous rain. We hunted in fog. Another morning we awoke to walk through grass covered meadows thick with frost. We saw it all! And best of all we shared the reality of a dream fulfilled.

The five of us brought three bull elk off that mountain. A young bull, a four by four, and a huge five by five with massive ivory tipped antlers. He looks just splendid looking down at me from a high wall in my living room.

Then I skipped a year to catch my breath and enjoyed the fall season doing all the fall things I had done near my home for over a half century. By the fall of 2000 plans were laid to explore the vast prairie pothole region of North Dakota.

Three eager duck hunters and two retrievers ventured into the rolling prairie country of the western Great Plains in quest of new duck hunting adventures. And we were not disappointed! We found friendly farmers, nearly unlimited open lands on which to hunt, ducks by the zillions, and a total absence of other waterfowl hunters!

Our first pilgrimage to the potholes in the plains resulted in a decision to make that trip an annual event. And it didn't take long for our numbers to swell.

In 2001, my dear friend of fifty-seven years, Eddie, joined our ranks, raising the human total to four. A year later another of my deer hunting buddies jumped on board. Now there were five. By October of 2003, two more additional bodies caused our vehicle count to jump to three, in order to haul what I refer to as "The Not so Magnificent Seven" and all our gear, plus five dogs, to our destination. The permanent membership of the Dakota bound Wisconsinites is now locked at our present numbers. The trailer house we rent out on the prairie will hold no more bodies. So don't call us, we'll call you!

The western prairie pothole country is expansive. It extends from western South Dakota northward into Canada for a considerable distance and continues west well into eastern Montana. The region is without a doubt the greatest duck factory in North America.

For visitors like myself, who have lived in a highly rural forested area where viewing distances are very limited, ones first encounter with the nearly treeless plains is a shock! The land stretches out before your astonished eyes nearly unbroken from horizon to horizon. To many, the land appears to be barren. I've heard folks describe the plains as "ugly", or "homely", or "boring". But there is much beauty everywhere, but to see it one must actually look!

I've visited the Great Plains when the seemingly endless fields of wheat, sunflowers, soybeans, and peas create a patchwork quilt effect that dazzles the eyes. The wind produces waves in the fields of grain, which makes one imagine they are traveling through a sea of gold. Visits to the plains after the giant harvesting machines have completed the harvest leave patterns in the stubble fields that resemble a monstrous jig saw puzzle. The numerous potholes are surrounded with stately cattails, bulrushes and dozens of other colorful marsh plants, their names unknown to this illiterate biologist.

To those of you who have never viewed a prairie sunrise or sunset, - well, all I can say is "You've got to see it to believe it!" And if you're sharing a duck blind with a buddy and your retriever, the view and the emotion are just slightly better. The endless horizon projects a colorful dawn or dusk of such magnitude as to be nearly unbelievable. Comparing "normal sunrises and sunsets", such as what I'm used to seeing in my native state, could be compared to living with a small black and white TV and then switching to a sixty-inch color model!

Besides the memories of numerous morning hunts, my gray repository where memories reside contain countless others. Where do I begin?

Our prairie pothole gang does not "hunt hard" during our annual visits to the western plains. There is no need to do so. Getting your "daily limit" of birds is so low on our list of "wants", it doesn't even appear on the list. But there is no doubt that on any given day that feat could be accomplished if that was ones goal. And even the worst wing shooters among us frequently achieve that plateau quite often.

Our routine is simple. Rise at five a.m. Relax in our cozy, warm environment sipping coffee and organizing our gear. Feed the dogs. Relive yesterday's memories. Depart for the pothole of our choice by six-thirty. Shooting time begins somewhere around seven-thirty. Hunt till nine or ten at the latest. Head back to our rental trailer for a gut filling breakfast. Next, while one team cleans the morning harvest, a second team cleans the kitchen and sets the living quarters in order. Then comes nap time, for both men and dogs. We take turns planning an evening meal and preparing it. That spreads out the cooking chores. About twoish, maps are opened and vehicles filled with rested hunters depart to explore new areas for potential new potholes to hunt. And new potholes are never far away nor had to find.

Imagine parking a few hundred feet from a small prairie pothole, walking through a fringe of native vegetation to the water's edge, - and flush five thousand ducks, geese, swans, sand hill cranes, and numerous varieties of water and shore birds! It's a scene right out of National Geographic!

Imagine having several dozen snow-white swans circle the pothole where you are concealed, and then splash down just yards from your hiding place!

Imagine being able to select which species of duck you'd like to bag, while allowing numerous other species to pass within range unmolested!

Imagine hunting five or six mornings in a row and not seeing another group of waterfowl hunters and often not even hearing any other gunfire except that produced by your companions!

All of this and much more need not be simply imagined. It can become a reality in the prairie pothole country of the Western Plains!

What does a weeklong trip like this cost? Gasoline, two nights in a motel, five days and nights in a rented trailer, food, drink, license, snacks, ammunition, etc. - we can do all of this on a five to six hundred dollars per person budget!

But to be honest, not all waterfowl hunting areas in the prairie pothole country are under hunted. Near the so-called major population centers you will have competition. And early in the season often lots of competition. But by doing your homework, you can still find remote places such as the ones my gang has discovered. How long this personal paradise will continue as it is, is anyone's guess. More and more TV hunting shows and sporting magazines are touting the wonders of the prairie pothole region. And sooner or later, more hunters will surely show up in even the most out of the way places. In the meantime "The Not So Magnificent Seven" will continue to enjoy our discovery.

As I write this, the gang's day of departure for what will be our Fifth Annual Dakota Hunt is still a little over a month away. I've already made "the list", and started packing. I haven't told my two dogs about it yet, but my old veteran, Siah, is getting suspicious.

Belle

My first Black Lab, Duke, convinced me to be a lifelong "Lab Man" for the duration of my hunting career. Years ago I recall reading a comment from a writer, whose name now escapes me, that sums up the world of dogs with one simple statement, with which I totally agree. The author penned; "There are dogs and then there are Labradors".

Early on I devised a plan as to how I could keep a steady supply of quality retrievers on hand and avoid having to train and hunt with a new pup after the old dog was retired or had passed on to 'The Big Doghouse In The Sky". Fortunately, I formulated a simple plan, which are about the only type of plans I have success working with.

I came up with what I like to refer to as my "Overlap Theory". Buy a new pup while the aging veteran is still in fairly good shape and allow the pup to learn not only from Master, but also from the Old Pro. Simple and effective!

In the spring of 2003 my wife and I decided the time had come to secure a new Black Lab pup. My fifth such breed, Siah, was be ginning to show the riggers of old age, and her wisdom needed to be transferred to the next generation.

In mid-April we selected a black bundle of love and energy from a friend who raises Labs. There were five in the litter, and two had already been claimed. We decided on a frisky female, who quickly tugged on our heartstrings. We took her home and named her Belle.

****

It's funny in a way that we humans "forget" certain important facts about this and that when we haven't experienced a particular situation for a few years. And it had been more than a few years since Peggy and I had a pup in our home.

Sixteen years had evaporated since our last Lab pup entered our lives. That was Sadie. When she began the downhill slide called old age, we inherited Siah from our youngest daughter and son-in-law. Siah was about two years old at the time and had only been a part of a duck hunt once when she was but nine months old. The youngster had made a most difficult retrieve on a downed bluebill as though she had been doing just that for years. I knew the dog had a great heart and natural instincts to go with it. My son-in-law decided getting up early in the morning to hunt ducks was not his cup of tea, so I talked Wendy and Mike into transferring Siah to our home.

But now, with the addition of Belle, we had a new puppy to contend with, and one that was energized beyond anything my wife and I could recall! Housebreaking took longer than we remembered it should, although actually that training period was rather short. Then we tried to deal with the chewing! Shoes, slippers, gloves, socks, and nearly everything that wasn't nailed down or four feet off the floor. However, we were lucky with furniture. Those items seemed to be low on Belle's preferred list of "things I like to destroy".

But like nearly all Labs I've known, Belle was smart and an eager learner. On the negative side we discovered she was what is referred to "The Alpha Bitch" of the litter. Simply explained, she wanted to be the boss of the house. It mattered not that Siah was ten times her size with a considerable amount of seniority, or Bugsy the Beagle had a feisty streak in him, it matter not, Belle wanted to be in charge! She wanted the food in the other dog's dish. She wanted whatever dog toy the older dogs were in possession of, she wanted to be petted and fussed over above all others, she terrorized our tough old tomcat. We nicknamed her "The Belle from Hell".

On the positive side, the pup loved water. She took her first swim in Lost Creek's frigid waters in late April when she was but ten weeks old, and loved it!

With time, effort, and patience, coupled with a strict training schedule did, and always will, pay off. Ever so slowly our pup began to evolve into a dog.

The last Saturday in September rolled around and with it the opening of Wisconsin's duck season. Siah and Belle, plus our local game warden shared my blind on Lost Creek for yet another chapter in my very thick book of opening days. Belle was but seven months old, and although we'd done a ton of training retrieving sticks, balls and the "dummy", which had been fitted with a pair of ducks wings I had saved from the previous season, the little girl was confused by the frenzied activity of the actual hunt.

The hunt was good. We saw several hundred mallards and wood ducks that afternoon, but trying to pick drake mallards out of the fast flying large flocks so early in the season was difficult beyond the two shooter's abilities. We settled for a mallard apiece and four wood ducks. The crop of wild rice was extremely thick, making it impossible for a dog to see a bird on the water after it fell. Belle sat on the bank looking confused and watched Siah make all the retrieves. But I took time out from the hunt to let Belle get in some practical practice retrieving some of Siah's efforts, which I tossed back in the creek for Belle to fetch. This she did with vigor! I was pleased with the early progress!

I awoke at five a.m. on the first of October to discover a minor blizzard was ragging outside. What a wonderful discovery! By five forty five Siah, Belle and Master were canoeing downstream towards our blind on the creek. A winter wonderland surrounded us, as giant, fluffy snowflakes continued to fall steadily.

By six-fifteen, a half dozen oversized mallard decoys bobbed in an open patch of water some twenty yards form my blind as I sipped my first cup of hot coffee and two eager retrievers nuzzled my cold hand. Ducks or no ducks, I was having a delightful start to a new day.

The first two flocks of mallards plopped in to visit my fakes well before legal shooting time. Siah whimpered and whined while looking at me as if I had once again gone loco. Try as I may, I have never been able to communicate the "legal shooting time" concept to a retriever. Belle seemed to sense the upcoming drama, as she squirmed and wiggled next to her senior partner.

Only minutes after slipping three number four steel shot duck loads into my 870, the action began. I dropped a drake wood duck into the rice, which Siah eagerly began to pursue. The old gal had to struggle through the thick rice, and I wondered how much heavy exertion her failing hips could take. Belle, perched on top of a clump of leather leaf brush at the creek's edge, watched her companion's struggle.

The sound of air rushing over cupped wings brought my attention to what was rapidly descending towards my decoys. A lone mallard drake was spiraling down from the snowy sky, fully intent on landing for some breakfast. Old instincts took control and at the report of my shotgun the bird folded cleanly and fell with a splash into the rice on the far side of the creek.

Belle was already in full leap towards the cold water before I could manage to say "fetch". Her first solo retrieve went off without a hitch! Her memory of where the bird had fallen was flawless, and those young, strong legs parted the tangled stalks of wild rice like Moses had parted the Red Sea! Belle was back with the mallard before Siah returned with the wood duck! I was elated beyond belief! With one difficult retrieve, my pup had graduated from rookie to retriever!

I bagged one additional mallard and one wood duck before calling it a morning shortly after eight thirty. Although well short of a limit, that fact was of little consequence. The joy of seeing my new pup make her first retrieve was enough thrills for one morning. And after my birds were cleaned and placed in the freezer, breakfast would taste extra good!

On the fourth of October a three truck convoy, packed with over a ton of equipment, headed west towards North Dakota. The list of passengers included seven eager duck hunters and five excited retrievers. This was to be my forth-annual pilgrimage to the land of endless potholes, as it was Siah's. Belle was making her maiden voyage.

We spent the first night in Devils Lake, ND, and were settled into our trailer on the prairie by eleven a.m. the following morning. By two thirty in the afternoon, Tom, my first day partner, was putting out decoys while I set up our portable blind. We were setting up shop on a tiny outcropping of prairie gumbo nearly in the center of what resembles a lake more than a typical prairie pothole. The pond is nearly a mile in length and about a quarter mile wide. A very sparse growth of short weeds covers the tiny island, which is totally inadequate for concealing two hunters and two black dogs.

The island was literally covered with goose and duck feathers. Gobs of goose droppings were everywhere. As we readied for the hunt, Siah sniffed every square inch of ground while Belle completed several high-speed laps around the landmass at the water's edge.

The final finishing touch to our decoy spread involved the placing of Robo-Duck. Robo is a battery powered mechanical decoy, which is perched on top of a metal stake, a foot or two above the surface of the water. When the switch is flipped to the "on" position, the decoy's wings begin rotating rapidly. This motion often attracts ducks on days when there is little or no wind to give conventional decoys motion. And this was a flat calm afternoon!

My inquisitive pup stood in the water beside Tom and watched as Robo was properly placed. Then Tom flipped the switch!

Within a millisecond after Robo's wings were set in motion. Belle instantly levitated about a foot above the surface of the water and set a new world record in the twenty-yard dash. Once at Master's side she peered between the safety of my legs, with the hair on her back standing at attention, and began to bark franticlly.

It took several minutes to calm Belle down and several additional minutes for Tom and I to stop laughing! Another lesson in the life of a young retriever had been completed. When our convoy first converged on the lake, somewhere in the neighborhood of several thousand ducks, geese, swans and white pelicans had vacated the premises. We knew many of them would soon be returning, and once settled in our blinds the action was quick in coming.

I pondered the unanswered question of how Belle would react to downed birds now that nothing but open water lay before us. A brace of spoonbills answered the question. Tom and I each dropped our first birds of the afternoon, giving each dog a chance to get wet. Siah chose to pursue the one with a broken wing. As I watched her slowly close the distance between dog and duck I missed seeing Belle quickly, and professionally, retrieve the second bird.

Tom got my attention by shouting, "Good dog Belle, good dog!" I turned my gaze from watching my old pro at work just in time to see my new pup drop the second bird in front of our blind! Now I was sure I owned two good retrievers!

By four p.m. Tom and I were loading our canoe on my truck and stuffing our legal limit of twelve ducks in the back end along with our decoys and two wet dogs. All four of us were smiling.

On day two our group split up and hunted two different potholes. My two dogs and I obtained a new partner, which was Eddie. Tom, JR and his golden retriever, Rusty, formed a second team. The four of us ventured into new territory, which was a large circular pothole set in the bottom of a deep bowl like depression in the prairie.

Late on the previous afternoon we had discovered the pothole and flushed several thousand mallards, gadwalls and geese from its surface.

The rim of the pothole offered excellent concealment in many thick clumps of cattails and bulrushes, so choosing a natural blind was a simple task. The early morning temperature hovered in the mid-thirties, which was a welcome relief from the sun drenched, sweltering eighty three-degree afternoon we had endured just yesterday. The pre-dawn grayness gradually gave way to a typical spectacular prairie sunrise, which offered up brilliant hues of pink, orange, purple and yellow. A multitude of natural sounds from the wildlife that lives near a prairie pothole engulfed us as we waited for the opening bell, which was scheduled to ring at seven thirty seven.

The first few flights of ducks arrived well before shooting time, increasing our pulse rates and causing low whines from Siah. Belle squirmed on her leash and probably wondered why there was no gunfire. It was no doubt an age-old question silently wondered by countless thousands of retrievers over the past several centuries.

Our marksmanship was less than acceptable at the first group of mallards that ventured over our decoy spreads shortly after our guns were loaded. Tom and JR cleanly folded one bird and Eddie and I knocked down a second one, as the frightened flock fought for more altitude. Rusty made short work out of retrieving the first bird, but bird number two had fallen far from our blind and was making a beeline for the thick cattails across the two hundred yard wide pond.

Siah was already outward bound in hot pursuit, fighting her way through belly deep water and soft, gooey muck. Belle strained on her leash, watching her companion pursue the crippled mallard.

In her younger days the chase would have been a short one, with the duck losing. But Father Time and a massive injury to Siah's left front shoulder from a battle with a very large beaver, plus the arthritis in her aging hips left my Old Pro with but one good leg. The distance between dog and duck was ever widening. It was time to send in the reserves!

I unsnapped Belle's leash and pointed towards the departing duck, telling her to "GO GET THE BIRD".

A sleek greyhound would have lost the race. Belle passed Siah like she was standing still. The mallard, now realizing the rules of the game had changed, made a hasty retreat into a thick stand of cattails in mid-pond. Belle reached the location and plunged into the tangle of cattails, emerging seconds later with the limp body of the duck. (Possibly the bird died of fright?)

Looking back at Master, chest deep in water and looking mighty proud, Belle held her conquest in a typical pose. A round of cheers and applause erupted from our companions, who had watched the drama unfold. Then Siah arrived on the scene!

Probably miffed by her ego being damaged by the younger dog, Siah attempted to take possession of the limp mallard. Belle disagreed. For the next thirty seconds four hunters and Rusty were treated to a serious game of "Tug 'o War" between two black dogs, with the duck playing the role of the rope. While my three hunting buddies nearly laughed their heads off, I nearly yelled mine off.

"SIAH, DROP THAT BIRD! THAT'S BELLE'S DUCK!" Etc., etc. But in the end Belle offered up her respect to her senior partner and released her grip on the duck. Once back at the blind I gave my old girl a minor scolding, but chuckled while doing so. All was forgiven. As the remainder of the week drifted by, both dogs received plenty of opportunities to do their thing. Which they did often and well. My two dogs had one additional dispute over who owned a duck after both dogs made a long swim and reached a drifting giant northern greenhead at the same moment. Siah also won that battle and returned with the prize. Belle returned to shore with a mouth full of breast feathers.

All in all, the entire experience worked out very well. My faithful old Siah quite possibly made her final trip to North Dakota. At this time it's difficult to say if her body will be up to making her fifth trip to the land of endless potholes. Although there is no doubt her heart will be.

But the basic training for my newest retriever is over. And although there are bound to be a few glitches in the immediate future, all signs point to Belle became another in a long line of outstanding retrievers I've been highly privileged to own and love.

The bottom line about Belle is this. There is no way to dispute the fact I went to North Dakota with a pup and returned to Wisconsin a week later with a dog!

Epilog: "To All The Dogs I've Loved Before"

Somewhere along the line I know I've mentioned I'm a dog lover. And even if you don't remember me saying so, I think you've probably been able to read between the line in my previous rambling and realize I have a sincere fondness for "Man's Best Friend".

There certainly has been a batch of pooches in my life, and to be honest, I have fonder feelings about some than others. Dogs, like the gin martinis I've consumed, were all good, but some just a tad better than others.

While I was still in diapers, my folks had two "Heinz 57" varieties, Jip and Chum. There is little stored in my gray matter that is the repository of memories about those two hounds, other than they followed me around a great deal and liked to lick my fingers after I had eaten something.

Next, from age five to eighteen two black cocker spaniels came into my life, Pat and Pat II. They were smart, obedient, good hunters, and friendly to family members. But like most of their breed had that cocky cocker temperament. As a youngster, those two were frequently my only playmates and companions during my formative years when I spent a considerable amount of time getting acquainted with Ma Nature. I loved both of those floppy eared black dogs dearly!

Duke was number five in the steady progression of dogs who took up residence in the Anderson household. I've devoted an entire chapter about that wonderful Lab, so I need not bother with repetitious remembrances concerning our nearly eleven-year love affair spanning 1963 through 1973.

Teal was adopted into our family in 1966. Peggy, and our two maturing offspring, and myself, had moved back to Wisconsin from Florida on a permanent basis and were not really in the market for a second dog. We rented a small log house a few miles from my boyhood home and spent the summer of '66 there before buying the family resort from my mom and then moving once again.

While at our rental unit we discovered our neighbors across the street were also in the process of moving. But they, unlike us, were moving a considerable distance from St. Germain, Wisconsin and had a young female black Lab to "get rid of". How could we refuse a bargain such as that?

Teal was one hundred and eighty degrees opposite of Duke. Duke was a large male, slightly bullheaded, (as according to my mom, all males are), and somewhat aggressive and intimidating towards strangers. Especially if they approached my truck, or in Duke's opinion posed a treat to any member of our family.

Teal, on the other hand, was a small female, willing to accept and complete any command at an instant, and laid back to such an extent I suspected that as a pup she may have been slightly abused.

Duke was such a positive presence in the field that it prevented Teal from reaching her potential as a retriever for several seasons. In fact, I had almost given up on her ever becoming a quality hunting dog. But when Duke's strength and stamina began to slide downhill, Teal's attitude and skills multiplied dramatically. And after Duke was no longer part of the team, Teal blossomed into a wonderful hunting dog. Her water retrieves were as good as it gets. Among the five black Labs I've owned, prior to Belle, (whose rating is still up in the air), Teal was the second best upland game bird dog of the bunch. From 1974 to her death on December 31, 1979, she gave me one hundred and ten percent!

On the date mentioned above, Teal died from a fatal heart attack as I was leading a group of friends towards a nearby swamp for an early winter hare hunt. She suddenly collapsed as she walked by my side, and died in my arms.

The event so touched my heart and soul that I wrote a story about the events leading up to that last fateful day. The story was published in an outdoor tabloid in 1980 and republished in the January/February 2002 issue of "Sporting Tales" magazine. I have also included the story in another of my upcoming books, "Just Some Damn Good Fishing and Hunting Tales".

Teal's demise left me without a Labrador, although Bunny the Beagle and one of her mixed breed Lab/Beagle pups, "Piddles", helped fill the void for several months. (The "hybrid" pup, which my three daughters named "Piddles" for obvious reasons, was one of five surprises created by an illicit love affair between my beagle and a neighbor's black Lab stud.)

The temporary void created by Teal's death was unexpectedly filled with the arrival of Maggie. Maggie was a two and a half-year-old female who belonged to one of my long time friends and guiding clients. Mr. Black was in the business of raising Labs to be trained as Seeing Eye Dogs for the visually impaired. As a pup, Maggie flunked out of Seeing Eye Dog School and was sent off to a prestigious dog school noted for training retrievers. There she graduated with honors!

Maggie's owner already had a personal hunting Lab, a wonderful big male named Buck, so Maggie became a pampered kennel dog. That was until my friend was notified of Teal's sudden death.

Maggie arrived by airfreight at the Rhinelander, Wisconsin airport in mid-January. She was a prisoner in a large dog travel kennel, which was loaded into the rear of my station wagon. We were strangers to each other and I had no idea what her reaction would be to our first personal encounter.

Maggie appeared to be very nervous as we departed the airport parking lot, and suddenly it dawned on me that having been cooped up in her kennel for who know how many hours, the poor girl had to go potty! I stopped my car, opened the rear door of my station wagon and let her out. Boy oh boy did she have to go! Now I wasn't sure if I'd convince her to get back in the car or not. But I had come prepared for that eventuality!

Nestled in my jacket pocket, wrapped in aluminum foil, was a large, juicy chunk of fried venison. I called, she came. I gave her the meat, which she took gently, and then wolfed it down in one gulp. I opened the front passenger side door and commanded, "Maggie, get in. You and I are going to your new home." And in she jumped. Our friendship had been bonded and it was all up hill from there.

Once home it took a few days for Bunny and Piddles to accept her, and visa versa, but good pals they did become. Maggie was a tough cookie, very aggressive in the field, but an outstanding retriever. Her temperament was much more like that of a male than a female, but then again, like people, no two dogs are alike.

Maggie gave me eight wonderful years of her life, but an unfortunate accident resulted in my having to put her down before her time. (The details of which would add nothing to this narrative.)

Maggie, may you rest in peace!

The same wonderful friend, who had so graciously given me Maggie, presented my son and I with Lab pups in the early fall of 1987. These were two more dogs that had been destined to become Seeing Eye Dogs but their careers were altered to become excellent retrievers. I had first pick of the pair and the one I selected became known as "Sadie". My son, Chris, named Sadie's sister "Morgan". (At the time my son had a crush on the starlet Morgan Fairchild.)

If I had to choose one overall favorite Lab out of my first five, Sadie would be the winner by a narrow margin. If ever a name fit a dog is was Sadie, as Sadie was in all respects a dignified, beautiful lady. Training her to obey came easier than falling off a chair. For example, it took but one ten-minute lesson for her to MASTER the command, "heal". One trip down my quarter mile driveway and back again was all it took! Unbelievable!

Sadie was very laid back, showing little emotion about most things (except being close to master) until a shotgun appeared. Then it was all business! Most all Labs are natural born retrievers, but Sadie's skills were well beyond any other dog I've ever owned or hunted with. Teaching her hand signals came almost as easily as the "heal" lesson.

It has been my experience that in general, retrievers tend to hunt too far ahead of the hunters when being used for finding upland game birds. Not Sadie. If she strayed more than twenty yards ahead, all I had to say was, "Easy girl", and she'd stop, look back, smile, and slow the pace. She was methodical during her search patterns for any specie of upland game birds or downed waterfowl.

Sadie learned the ins and outs of upland game bird hunting using ruffed grouse and woodcock as her teachers. But it wasn't until she was seven before I was able to take her on a pheasant hunt. I was invited to be the fifth person on an early December pheasant hunt in southwestern Iowa. Besides Sadie, there were two veteran Springer Spaniels on board. I was quite apprehensive as to how my virgin pheasant dog would stack up against the two old pros. I was not to be disappointed!

At the end of our first days hunt, as my companions and I were nestled before a crackling fire in our rented quarters ingesting a glass or two of internal body stimulants, one of the gentlemen questioned where I had hunted pheasants with Sadie in past seasons. The individual nearly dropped his glass of chilled liquid when I told him this was her first experience afield for the colorful cacklers.

One incident that took place during that first Iowa pheasant hunt was so memorable the individual who was my partner on that day still talks about it, even though a decade and a half have evaporated since it occurred.

Tom and I were crossing a vast stubble field to become "blockers" at the end of a long, grass filled drainage ditch. Our three companions and the spaniels were a half-mile south of us, at the other end of the drainage ditch. Once Tom and I reached our appointed positions, our partners were to "make a drive" along the twisting course of the waterway.

Fifty yards short of the ditch, Sadie, who had been following along behind me, suddenly put her nose to the ground and began following what evidently was a hot scent. Tom and I now became the followers. My dog led us to the edge of the drainage ditch, plunged into the tangled grass and promptly flushed a rooster.

My shot was taken through heavy alders, which lined the banks of the ditch, but enough of the shot pattern found its mark and the rooster tumbled cleanly. Sadie was at the crash site several seconds later, and with head held high and proud galloped back towards her master. Tom remarked, "Nice shot!"

As my retriever neared the far edge of the cover along the ditch, still holding the freshly killed pheasant, she suddenly made a left turn and plunged into the thick grass. A second rooster rocketed skyward. The range of this second bird was much further than the first one, but amidst a shower of alder toothpicks, several of my number sixes found their mark. The rooster went down with a broken wing and the chase was on!

Sadie dropped the first bird and took off in hot pursuit. The race was rather one sided, and for the second time in less than a minute my beautiful shiny black dog was bringing her master the fruits of our labors.

The mystery was, how could a dog with a face full of feathers still be able to detect the scent of another similar bird at a range of ten or more yards? But that was my Sadie, and she was very special!

Sadie starred in another leading role a year later. Working together on the opening day of woodcock season we bagged a rare limit of five birds, which included my second "double on doodles". That special memory was recorded and appeared as a feature story in the July/August 2001 edition of "Sporting Tales" magazine.

Sadie's last two retrieves took place in December of 1998. Sadie, Siah and I were members of a small group of pheasant hunters who were spending two days combing the fields of a private farm located in Central Wisconsin. Being a "release and hunt" farm, the birds were numerous.

Sadie did well the first afternoon, but was limping badly on the morning of the second day. Her age and arthritis had caught up to her. But like all great retrievers, her heart was still strong and her spirit was willing.

Siah and two Chessies roamed ahead in a field of tall standing corn, while Sadie slowly trudged behind her master. Far to our left a bird flushed, followed by a volley of shotgun blasts. The bird went down with a broken wing and the chase was on. Sadie and I stopped and waited for the three dogs that were at the crash site to locate the wounded bird. Five minutes passed. No bird, but much shouting and yelling at the birdless threesome. It was time to call the bullpen for a reliever retriever.

I walked my Old Pro over to the assembled multitude of hunters and dogs and inquired as to where they suspected the pheasant had fallen. Several feathers marked the location. Sadie put her educated nose to the ground, gave a couple of loud sniffs, and started trailing the lingering scent. Thirty feet further she stopped at a hole under the roots of a stalk of corn and began pawing. I kneeled down and peered into the cavity. There was Mr. Rooster! Sadie actually smirked as she passed the younger dogs with the bird in her mouth. The three canine onlookers seemed to be embarrassed.

Later that morning I took a long shot at a rooster who flushed well ahead of the dogs. I detected a slight hesitation in its wing beat, but the bird continued to fly strongly away and sailed over a row of aspen trees which separated the field we were hunting from the one beyond it.

"I hit that bird!", I loudly announced to my comrades in arms.

One of the group responded. "Oh sure you did! NOT!" (Some people are simply disbelievers.)

After finishing out the field we proceeded to the next one where the bird I had shot at had settled in. I convinced my colleagues to help me look for the downed rooster. I was sure he had been body shot and was probably lying dead somewhere in the tangle of sorghum before us. But my buddies were highly skeptical of my claim and quickly called off their dogs, gave up the search, and moved on.

Being slightly bullheaded myself, at least at times like this, I kept Siah and Sadie on what was looking more and more like a fruitless search for the rooster. Five minutes later I admitted defeat and decided to call it quits and catch up with my companions. Maybe, just maybe, I was wrong in my assumption that a couple of my number 6's had found their mark.

I called for my two dogs. Siah responded almost immediately. Another minute ticked away as I waited for my faithful Sadie to appear. No dog. I called again. Moments later the sorghum wigged a bit and out into the pathway limped the Old Pro. And in her mouth was a dead rooster!

She slowly and painfully made her way to my side and professionally laid the bird at my boots. Then she turned her graying muzzle upward, looked me right in the eye,- and so help me, - she winked! This, her final retrieve marked the end of the play. The fat lady had sung!

Father Time continued to take his toll, and on Mother's Day in May of 1999, I laid my fourth black Lab to rest in our pet cemetery on the hill behind our home. Like all those before her, Sadie had joined her predecessors who's spirits now watch over the valley below, which had been their home.

As indicated in the preceding tale, Siah became a member of our household at age two, after being adopted from our youngest daughter and son-in-law. Siah learned much from Sadie, but had a much more aggressive attitude towards hunting in general. And although that's a good thing, her over eagerness resulted in having an upland game dog that needed the restraint of a training collar in some situations. As a water retriever she was top drawer!

However, Siah reached her tenth birthday on January 19, 2004, and doubts linger in my mind if she'll be able to withstand the rigors of any prolonged hunts come fall. She'll probably make my annual prairie pothole hunt in October, but it most likely will be her last trip to the land of endless potholes.

So that leaves Belle. Belle will no doubt be my last hunting dog. By the time she is ready for retirement, so probably will be her master. The years have slipped by all too rapidly, but I certainly have no complaints about the amount of time and the massive amount of cherished memories I've been allowed to store for what hopefully will be my really old age.

I still look forward to "next season", fully realizing each and every one could be my last. It goes without saying that besides all the "firsts" in our lives, there will also be many "lasts". But until that last hunt comes, Belle and I are going to enjoy each and every one we share, as we continue to watch the skies, - in the company of cattails, speckled alders and golden tamaracks!

"There was something of the boy about him which most men pretend to outgrow, and, doing so, thus become old."

Gordon MacQuarrie

About The Author

Leon "Buckshot" Anderson has spent the better part of six decades living in and being a part of the great out of doors. He began guiding fisherpersons when he was fourteen, and achieved such a degree of professionalism as an outdoorsman, he was honored by being inducted into the National Freshwater Fishing Hall of Fame as a "Legendary Guide" in 2001

Writing has been one of his passions since boyhood and many of his stories and tales have been published in numerous outdoor publications and newspapers. Besides "Cattails, Speckled Alders and Golden Tamaracks", he has authored three additional books "Last of a Dying Breed", "Growing Up Isn't All Fishing and Hunting", and "Evil, Veiled by Darkness".

He also writes weekly and monthly outdoor columns for two local newspapers.

www.ingramcontent.com/pod-product-compliance
Lightning Source LLC
Chambersburg PA
CBHW020438290526
45785CB00002B/911